Marriage

Other Books of Related Interest

Opposing Viewpoints Series

Current Controversies Series

At Issue Series

GLOBALVIEWPOINTS

| Marriage

Alicia Cafferty Lerner, Book Editor

GREENHAVEN PRESS
A part of Gale, Cengage Learning

GALE
CENGAGE Learning

Detroit • New York • San Francisco • New Haven, Conn • Waterville, Maine • London

Christine Nasso, *Publisher*
Elizabeth Des Chenes, *Managing Editor*

For more information, contact:
Greenhaven Press
27500 Drake Rd.
Farmington Hills, MI 48331-3535
Or you can visit our Internet site at gale.cengage.com

For product information and technology assistance, contact us at

Gale Customer Support, 1-800-877-4253
For permission to use material from this text or product, submit all requests online at www.cengage.com/permissions

Further permissions questions can be emailed to permissionrequest@cengage.com

Articles in Greenhaven Press anthologies are often edited for length to meet page requirements. In addition, original titles of these works are changed to clearly present the main thesis and to explicitly indicate the author's opinion. Every effort is made to ensure that Greenhaven Press accurately reflects the original intent of the authors. Every effort has been made to trace the owners of copyrighted material.

Cover photograph © Cindy Hughes, 2008. Used under license from Shutterstock.com.

LIBRARY OF CONGRESS CATALOGING-IN-PUBLICATION DATA

Marriage / Alicia Cafferty Lerner, book editor.
    p. cm. -- (Global viewpoints)
    Includes bibliographical references and index.
    ISBN 978-0-7377-4160-5 (hardcover)
    ISBN 978-0-7377-4161-2 (pbk.)
    1. Marriage. I. Lerner, Alicia Cafferty.
    HQ734. M35 2009
    306.8109--dc22

                                                                   2008035524

Printed in the United States of America
1 2 3 4 5 6 7 12 11 10 09 08

Contents

Chapter 1: Marriage and Human Rights Abuses

   In Malawi, Africa, an estimated 75 percent of wives experience marital rape. Gender activists have rallied to amend the domestic violence bill to include rape as a criminal offense.

   A girl from Niger was married at fourteen years of age and became pregnant just a year later. An improper cesarean section ripped her uterus, giving her a condition called a fistula. She now lives in isolation from her husband and village.

   The husband of a young Bangladeshi woman assaulted her for unknown reasons. He threw acid over her head, burning 20 percent of her body.

   Pooja, an Indian woman victim to her husband and in-laws' cruelty over dowry, protested by walking the streets of her city, Rajkot, in only her underwear. Her message is for her country to stop mistreating its women, particularly within the structure of marriage.

Chapter 2: Arranged Marriage, Child Marriage, and Polygamy

Chapter 3: Same-Sex Marriage

Chapter 5: Marriage and Sex

Foreword

*"The problems of all of humanity can
only be solved by all of humanity."*
—Swiss author Friedrich Dürrenmatt

Global interdependence has become an undeniable reality. Mass media and technology have increased worldwide access to information and created a society of global citizens. Understanding and navigating this global community is a challenge, requiring a high degree of information literacy and a new level of learning sophistication.

Building on the success of its flagship series, *Opposing Viewpoints*, Greenhaven Press has created the *Global Viewpoints* series to examine a broad range of current, often controversial topics of worldwide importance from a variety of international perspectives. Providing students and other readers with the information they need to explore global connections and think critically about worldwide implications, each *Global Viewpoints* volume offers a panoramic view of a topic of widespread significance.

Drugs, famine, immigration—a broad, international treatment is essential to do justice to social, environmental, health, and political issues such as these. Junior high, high school, and early college students, as well as general readers, can all use *Global Viewpoints* anthologies to discern the complexities relating to each issue. Readers will be able to examine unique national perspectives while, at the same time, appreciating the interconnectedness that global priorities bring to all nations and cultures.

Material in each volume is selected from a diverse range of sources, including journals, magazines, newspapers, nonfiction books, speeches, government documents, pamphlets, organization newsletters, and position papers. *Global Viewpoints* is truly global, with material drawn primarily from international sources available in English and secondarily from U.S. sources with extensive international coverage.

Features of each volume in the *Global Viewpoints* series include:

- An **annotated table of contents** that provides a brief summary of each essay in the volume, including the name of the country or area covered in the essay.

- An **introduction** specific to the volume topic.

- A **world map** to help readers locate the countries or areas covered in the essays.

- For each viewpoint, an **introduction** that contains notes about the author and source of the viewpoint explains why material from the specific country is being presented, summarizes the main points of the viewpoint, and offers three **guided reading questions** to aid in understanding and comprehension.

- **For further discussion** questions that promote critical thinking by asking the reader to compare and contrast aspects of the viewpoints or draw conclusions about perspectives and arguments.

- A worldwide list of **organizations to contact** for readers seeking additional information.

- A **periodical bibliography** for each chapter and a **bibliography of books** on the volume topic to aid in further research.

- A comprehensive **subject index** to offer access to people, places, events, and subjects cited in the text, with the countries covered in the viewpoints highlighted.

Global Viewpoints is designed for a broad spectrum of readers who want to learn more about current events, history, political science, government, international relations, economics, environmental science, world cultures, and sociology—students doing research for class assignments or debates, teachers and faculty seeking to supplement course materials, and others wanting to understand current issues better. By presenting how people in various countries perceive the root causes, current consequences, and proposed solutions to worldwide challenges, *Global Viewpoints* volumes offer readers opportunities to enhance their global awareness and their knowledge of cultures worldwide.

Introduction

The evolution of marriage has been quite extensive since its
ancient origins. Changing perceptions of morality, the social regulator that Irish playwright George Bernard Shaw per-
sonified through Victorian characters, have greatly stimulated
the evolution of marriage. Studying the progression and di-
gression of this legal union, through different moral climates,
allows for an understanding of what aspects have changed, in-
tensified, and loosened in global societies. This introduction
will glimpse at the institution of marriage in two different
global locations and social climates that have been challenged
by social and moral beliefs: the tightening of morals in Victorian England and questioning of morals in contemporary
South Africa.

England's Victorian Era (1837–1901) has become synony-
mous with sexual prudery both inside and outside the con-
fines of marriage. An example of the Victorian extremes in
promoting modesty reached well beyond women's practice of
clothing themselves neck to ankle: to prevent a man's mind
from wandering to the thought of a woman's naked leg, pi-
anos in home parlors often had their legs clothed. Such aspects of Victorian prudery were mocked by satirists and writ-
ers of the time, such as Oscar Wilde, who painted a picture of

the absurdity of the Victorian aristocratic ideals of love and marriage in his comedy of manners *The Importance of Being Earnest*.

The material for satires on Victorian marriages was rich, often inflecting the contradictions and hypocrisy of the Victorians' views on marriage and sexuality. While the wives were educated to be as modest as possible, many of their husbands sought prostitutes, often returning home with sexually transmitted diseases such as syphilis. This was a vicious cycle in many English marriages of the time, because husbands and wives did not discuss the topic of sex within the home.

Victorian marriages in England expected men and women to marry within their social classes. This revolved around the aristocratic system, starting with the queen and descending to English peasantry. Many Victorians, especially women who were brought up through a genteel education, held marriage on a pedestal. Victorian author Jane Austen's novel *Pride and Prejudice* lists the accomplishments of an eligible woman through the character Caroline: "A woman must have a thorough knowledge of music, singing, drawing, dancing, and the modern languages. . . ." It was through this education of manners that morality in marriage was reinforced, and the ideal of a proper marriage held the imagination of many women who were bred for its purpose and discouraged from being as educated as their male counterparts.

The pressures to marry within class for romantic and moral reasons provoked a trend toward spinsterhood (women remaining single) for a number of Victorian women in England. They were hesitant—or even defiant—to lose their autonomy in a marriage and often didn't agree with the social conditioning of men and women and the moral contradictions that Victorian England fostered. In the face of such women moving toward autonomy, the socialized Victorian message made clear that women and men were fundamentally different: The man was the provider and the woman, as the picture of morality, was often referred to as the angel of the house. Many often mocked spinsters, calling them "old maids," and treating them as outcasts. The philosophies behind spinsterhood were often based on the belief that women should simply retain their identities in a society ruled by a moral mold rather than by freethinkers. This was too radical for English Victorians, a society under magnified morality.

Gender roles and ideals of morality continue to play a part in modern views of marriage.

When South Africa was first faced with the adoption of same-sex marriage in 2006, many traditionalists questioned who would take the part of the groom and who would take the part of the bride in the marriage ceremony. Traditional South African wedding ceremonies are symbolic in their treatment of gender roles. Redefining the longstanding form of marriage between a man and woman in a wholly traditional and ceremonial country has been challenging what South Africans believe to be moral. As the Victorian spinsters often rebuked the tradition of marriage, causing controversy in an otherwise "don't ask, don't tell" society, South Africa's tug of war with morality over the issue of same-sex marriage has been, and remains, controversial.

Though a country with traditional morals about sexuality, South Africa is not new to liberal politics. In 1994, after the end of apartheid (the legal racial segregation in South Africa from 1948–1994), South Africa made it a priority to dismiss laws that upheld discrimination of any kind. South Africa became the first country in the world to hold a constitution that prohibited the discrimination of people based on their sexuality. This did not include the right of same-sex marriage at the time, but its meaning put fuel to fire for activists in favor of its legalization.

The controversy of same-sex marriage in South Africa has come from several corners. Many traditionalist citizens and politicians believe it rebukes socialized African cultural norms.

Similar to the Victorian philosophy, many traditionalists in South Africa feel that "normal" aspects of a society, such as gender roles, should be upheld for the good of the people.

Controversy is also stirred by religions. Because religions are often held as moral authorities by their followers, they are a major influence for many people. Muslim groups and the Roman Catholic Church, among other religious groups, have disagreed with the law, believing it to clash with the sanctity of marriage.

In contrast, many of South Africa's same-sex marriage supporters believe that South Africa's history of apartheid should teach tolerance among differences including race, culture, or sexual orientation. The marriage amendment has made same-sex marriage legal in South Africa, but that does not eliminate intolerance including hate crimes experienced by some gays and lesbians. South Africa is the only country in Africa to have legalized same-sex marriage. Many surrounding countries do not discuss its existence, let alone tolerate it, and have been known to ridicule South Africa for not being truly "African" by allowing an amendment that confuses gender norms. Hate crimes and other forms of outward intolerance based on sexual orientation are always immoral.

Victorian England was a period that tightened the ropes on sexuality, making it taboo, and upheld a moral mold of marriage that was not greatly challenged by its aristocratic society. In contrast, contemporary South Africa is a country with deep-rooted, often ancient traditions that are very much alive in a society that is experiencing great changes in equality. Once ruled by various European aristocracies, its fight for democracy has paved the way for an evolution of its people and new developments in the institution of marriage.

Global Viewpoints: Marriage examines numerous issues associated with the legal union of marriage today. The authors present different perspectives from around the world on various subjects such as marital rape, dowry abuse, arranged marriage, child marriage, polygamy, debates on same-sex marriage, financing marriage, prenuptial agreements, sexless marriage, and adultery. Throughout history, and still today, marriage is a union that is both personal and public. What happens behind closed doors is often echoed around the globe with opinions of what is and is not just, moral, and free. It is no wonder that different forms of this institution have been glorified and scrutinized. The face of marriage today is a reflection of its textured history. To some it is a colorless, sexless human right, while others consider it a formality based on religion and culture. Such questions have and will always surround this institution. Our present generation, as generations before, will undoubtedly make its mark in the evolution of marriage for future generations to interpret.

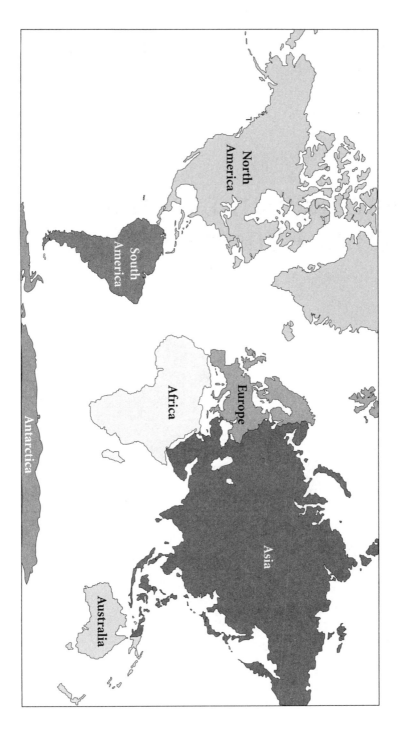

CHAPTER 1

Marriage and Human Rights Abuses

Malawi's Gender Activists Expose Marital Rape

Hobbs Gama

In the following viewpoint, Hobbs Gama discusses the issue of marital rape in Malawi, Africa. According to Gama, some Malawian women are campaigning for an amendment to the domestic violence bill that would include marital rape as a crime. Gama recognizes that many Malawian men do not believe that rape can exist between a husband and wife and fear that if rape is included in domestic violence laws, many men will go to prison, and divorce rates will rise. Gama is a reporter for New African, *a monthly news magazine headquartered in London, England.*

As you read, consider the following questions:

1. According to the author, what percentage of women makes up Malawi's 12 million population?
2. As stated by the author, what is the punishment for rape in Malawi?
3. As quoted by Gama, what reason does lawyer John Katsala give as to why he believes that rape cannot exist within marriage?

The idea of a man raping his wife is unheard of in many parts of "traditional" Africa. Now it is all over the place in Malawi [located in southeastern Africa]. For the first time in

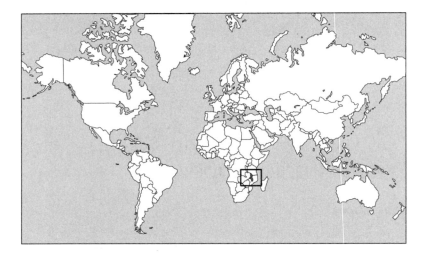

the country's history, gender activists from developed countries have sponsored the launch of a nationwide campaign for marital rape to be legislated against.

Slogans such as "breaking the silence" and "women standing for their rights and for fair play in marriage" are getting louder as the campaign rolls on. Now Malawian men fear that they would sooner or later be forced to adapt to the "imported" new language and demands of the gender activists.

Malawian Women Rally to Amend Domestic Violence Bill

It all started when ten Malawian women observed—from 25 November to 10 December last year [2001]—sixteen days of what they called "Activism Against Gender Violence"—an international campaign originating from the first women's Global Leadership Institute, sponsored by the Centre for Women's Global Leadership, in 1991.

Participants chose 25 November (the International Day Against Violence Against Women) and 10 December (the International Human Rights Day) in order to symbolically link violence against women and human rights.

Since the campaign, and with the support of the Women in Law in Southern Africa (WILSA), chapters of women's rights organisations in Malawi have held a series of meetings aimed at forcing the government to change certain "unfavourable sections" in the domestic violence bill that are deemed "not strong enough to protect the interests of women."

Government officials, MPs, traditional chiefs and church organizations were courted by the activists.

Anastasia Msosa, a renowned Malawi Supreme Court judge, said that although marital rape was sidelined as a gender-based human rights violation, "it does exist and women are suffering silently, letting it pass as a family or domestic matter."

According to a recent survey, 75% of Malawian wives are raped by their husbands.

She continued: "There is no need to run away from the truth. Marital rape is there. I support the inclusion of rape in the law that Parliament is about to put in place."

Women make up 52% of Malawi's 12 million population. A study carried out by the health ministry discovered that men routinely forced their spouses into sex when they were not willing, or not in the mood, sick or not interested.

Lilian Ngoma, the ministry's spokeswoman, confirmed: "The survey found that many women do not enjoy sex in their homes. Many have been in marriage for several years, they have children but never experienced an orgasm. It also revealed that 75% of wives are raped by the husbands."

Most Malawian Men Do Not Believe Rape Exists in Marriage

Malawian law provides for a six-year jail sentence for rape. Men fear that if marital rape was established, a lot of them could end up in jail, leading to unnecessary divorces.

Africans Debate the Existence of Marital Rape

The UN [United Nations] Committee on the Elimination of Discrimination against Women asked Uganda in August 2002 to put in place measures to curb cases of violence against women, including marital rape. . . .

The UN experts observed Uganda had many incidents of "violence against women such as domestic violence, rape, including marital rape, incest, sexual harassment in the workplace and other forms of sexual abuse of women."

Participants in the Mbarara workshop [a workshop organized by the UN Office of the High Commissioner for Human Rights (OHCHR)] drawn from civic, political and law enforcers in western region sharply disagreed on whether marital rape should be an offence in Uganda.

Some male participants said marital rape should be changed to "marital sexual violence", while some females disagreed. . . .

Mid-western police chief, Martin Amoru, said the police normally turns away spouses that approach it with such complaints.

"There is no law for marital rape in our books, so long as the married couple uses the right organs in their home, there is no offence," he said, attracting a protracted debate.

OHCHR's representative in Uganda, Maarit Kohonen, disagreed with the policeman.

"The law on rape should take on the act itself rather than the players, whether they are married or not," she said. "Rape at any point will be considered a crime. These things [marital rape] need to be investigated and dealt with."

Solomon Muyita and Felix Basiime, "Does Rape Exist in Marriages?"
The Monitor (Kampala), November 2, 2007.

"I don't think it is proper to say a man raped his wife," says John Katsala, a lawyer from Malawi's Law Commission. "Marriage and rape cannot go together, because you have to satisfy each other. It is even there in the Bible."

Katsala's view is shared by most Malawian men, especially those in the legal profession who have strongly criticised the women activists for "importing legislation from developed countries."

Duncan Tambala, another Supreme Court judge, argues: "If 75% of men rape their wives, the same percentage would have to be slapped with a jail sentence as rapists—which would mean the fall of the family in Malawi."

But Anetta Chawanje, a social worker with a children's rights NGO [nongovernmental organization] in Nsanje district, southern Malawi, disagrees. "Men have a problem with the language. They do not want the word 'rape' to appear in the new domestic law. But even if another word is used, marital rape still deserves a stiffer punishment."

Now even the African bedroom is no longer immune to globalisation.

Niger's Child Marriages Have Dangerous Consequences

Sabine Dolan

In the following viewpoint, Sabine Dolan argues about the harsh consequences of allowing young girls to marry in places such as Niger, which has the highest rate of child marriage in the world. Dolan reports on the story of Habiba, a Nigerian girl married when she was fourteen years old. Dolan explains an improper caesarian section ripped Habiba's uterus, giving her a painful condition called a fistula, after which her husband left her and her village shunned her. Dolan is a correspondent for UNICEF. UNICEF, the United Nations Children's Fund, addresses such issues as the need to empower girls through education and the recognition of children's rights.

As you read, consider the following questions:

1. What is the author's definition of a *fistula*?
2. According to Dolan, what is one of the main reasons girls' educations are cut short?
3. What does the author claim to be the reason for Souba's father postponing her wedding?

Habiba, now 17, lives in a small village in southern Niger's Tibiri region. Married three years ago [2004], she has since endured a tragedy that illustrates some of the worst perils of early marriage.

Sabine Dolan, "Habiba's Story: Early Marriage Leads to Tragedy for a Young Woman in Niger," UNICEF, May 29, 2007. Reproduced by permission.

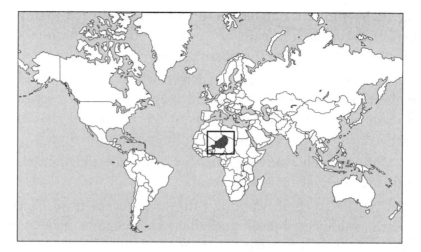

"I was given in marriage when I turned 14," says Habiba. "At that time I was healthy. I became pregnant one year after the marriage. I was in labour for two days and was transferred to a regional hospital where I had a caesarean. That's when I suffered a fistula."

A botched caesarean ripped her small uterus, allowing leakage of urine and feces into the vagina—a condition known as [a] fistula. Habiba's fistula left her with chronic incontinence and pain. She lost her baby hours after he was born.

> *"By 15, half of all girls are married, and most begin having children within two years."*

But Habiba's ordeal didn't stop here. After the disastrous delivery, her husband left her and the village rejected her. Today she lives alone with her mother. Ostracized and humiliated, she no longer ventures outside her house, not even to get water.

Highest Incidence of Early Marriage

Habiba's mother, Zeinabou Mahaman, 45, explains that her daughter sometimes wakes up from the pain in the middle of the night. She says Habiba has to spend a lot of time washing herself to soothe the pain, to cool her off from the intense heat and to make sure she doesn't smell.

This fate is not unusual in Niger, which has the world's highest incidence of early marriage and where, on average, women bear seven children each. By 15, half of all girls are married, and most begin having children within two years.

Unfortunately, young women who become pregnant this early are especially at risk of fistula.

UNICEF has been working with the government of Niger, as well as influential traditional chiefs and religious leaders, to raise the minimum marriage age for girls to 18 and to support their access to health care and education. This latter point is critical because early marriage is one of the main obstacles to a girl's education. Once married, most girls drop out of school.

Village Awareness Campaign

Just a few houses away from Habiba lives Soueba, 14.

Soueba was promised into marriage but, her mother explains, the girl's father delayed the wedding after attending a village awareness campaign about the dangers of early marriage and then hearing about Habiba's fistula.

Hadiza Saidou, 47, Soueba's mother, married young and gave birth to seven children. She says she was always against her daughter's early marriage.

"I strongly opposed it," she explains. "One of my own sisters became handicapped for life soon after her wedding as a result of a difficult pregnancy at a young age."

Soueba says she was relieved when her father finally changed his mind. "I'm really happy and moved to have escaped from my marriage. My neighbour's situation and the horrible consequences of her wedding speak for themselves. God saved me!"

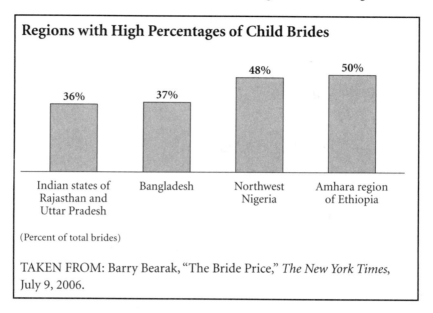

Regions with High Percentages of Child Brides

Indian states of Rajasthan and Uttar Pradesh	Bangladesh	Northwest Nigeria	Amhara region of Ethiopia
36%	37%	48%	50%

(Percent of total brides)

TAKEN FROM: Barry Bearak, "The Bride Price," *The New York Times*, July 9, 2006.

'My Dream Is to Be Cured'

For her part, Habiba dreams of resuming a normal life.

"My dream is to heal," she says. "I no longer have any contacts with anybody because they show their disgust with my smell. That's why my dream is to be cured."

UNICEF and its partners—including the nongovernmental organization Solidarité and the United Nations Population Fund—support surgical interventions for girls like Habiba, while UNICEF also helps them reintegrate into their communities.

For now, her mother prays for Habiba, who is scheduled to have restorative surgery in the coming months.

Bangladeshi Bride's Future Stunted by Acid Abuse

Mahbuba Zannat

In the following viewpoint, Mahbuba Zannat argues that al-though acid violence has considerably diminished during recent years, it remains a reality for some women and children in Bangladesh. Zannat reports the story of Nila, an eighteen-year-old Bangladeshi girl, who was the victim of acid abuse by her husband. According to Zannat, campaigns and acts against acid violence have helped to improve the situation, but they have not eradicated this violence, as witnessed in Nila's experience. Zan-nat is a reporter for The Daily Star *based in Bangladesh.*

As you read, consider the following questions:

1. According to the author, what year did the government pass two acts to prevent acid violence?
2. As cited by the author, what percentage of the 1,400 burn patients seen in a year's time by the Dhaka Medi-cal College Hospital burn unit are acid victims?
3. As acknowledged by the author, plastic and reconstruc-tive surgery consultant, Ronald W. Hiles, said acid vio-lence was reduced by how much since 2002?

Young bride Nila's dreams have been shattered the night her husband poured down acid on her, burning her face, hands and other parts of the body.

Mahbuba Zannat, "Dream Burnt in Acid," *The Daily Star*, March 2, 2008. www.the dailystar.net. Reproduced by permission.

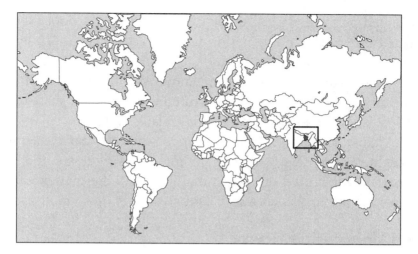

The barbaric act has landed the critically injured 18-year-old girl in a hospital bed of Acid Survivors Foundation (ASF) with no hope of taking the Secondary School Certificate examinations due next month.

No Reason Behind the Violence

Nila cannot think of any explainable reason why the man who tied the knot with her a year ago would even do such an act that would put her life in danger.

Her parents arranged the marriage with Akbar Hossain, 30, a Saudi Arabian expatriate back then.

"It wasn't for dowry and we didn't even quarrel with each other. I know he is a short-tempered man. He got angry with me for some reason, but I don't understand why," said a baffled Nila while groaning with agonising pain in her bed.

A Newly Wed Teenager with Aspirations of Performing Arts

This teenage schoolgirl from Baro Bashoria village in Sirajganj [Bangladesh] had a passion for performing arts and cherished a dream of becoming established in the field someday. This talented performer used to win awards from her school every year for her outstanding performance in acting, singing, poem recitation and dance.

"The man to whom we handed over our beloved daughter with the hope that he would nurture her dream, has shattered it instead," Nila's mother said with a blank look.

"Akbar seemed to be a polite man when we arranged our daughter's marriage with him. Who could've guessed that a man like him could do something like this?" the mother said while talking to this correspondent at the ASF hospital.

An Unexpected Horror

"On February 19, my husband got very upset at me as I wanted to go to my parents'. I tried to settle the matter, but he didn't calm down. After we had the dinner, he left for the market, but I didn't know why. He didn't even come to bed later," recalled Nila.

"I woke up around midnight and found my husband sitting on a chair with his eyes bloodshot out of anger. I asked him what had happened, but no response. He just walked up to me with a glassful of liquid and poured it down over my head," Nila said reminiscing the dreadful night.

"I suddenly felt an excruciating burning sensation over my entire face and my arms, realising that it was acid. My husband rushed out of the house right after that," she added.

"I received the first treatment 20 hours later after my father brought me to Dhaka Medical College Hospital [DMCH]," Nila said.

"221 women and children fall victim to acid violence every year."

She was later transferred to the ASF hospital. Doctors at ASF hospital said her face and eyes have been damaged badly and 20 percent of her body was burned in the acid attack.

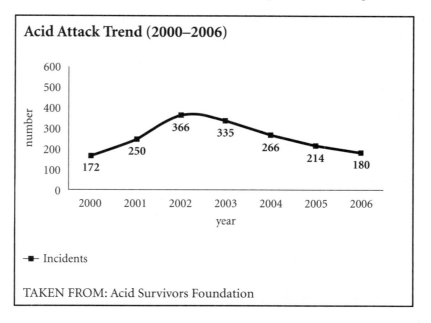

Acid Attack Trend (2000–2006)

TAKEN FROM: Acid Survivors Foundation

They fear she might even go blind. "Nila came to our hospital in a critical condition with deep burns that involved her vital organs. Though we work with acid victims, we've seen only a few patients with such major burns," said Dr Sanjoy Biswas of ASF.

The Rise and Fall of Acid Violence

A large number of women and children fall victim to acid violence every year. According to an ASF report, on an average, 221 women and children fall victim to acid violence every year and the main causes of the violence are dowry, refusal of love proposal and land disputes.

According to the report, the number of persons attacked with acid came down to 187 in 2007 from 234 in 2000 and 349 in 2001. In 2006, the total number of acid victims was 221, the report stated.

The acid violence incidents saw a sharp rise in the '90s and started to decline in the decade that followed—thanks to the awareness campaigns, legal and rehabilitation assistance programmes taken up by different government and non-government organisations (NGOs).

The situation improved in 2002 when the government passed two acts for curbing and preventing the acid violence and started to work together with the NGOs.

The DMCH burn unit still treats 2 to 3 percent acid victims out of around 1,400 burn patients every year.

The number of acid violence has been declining gradually due to the enactment of the new laws and the campaigns of the government and the NGOs, said Dr Shamanta Lal Sen of Burn and Plastic Surgery Unit at DMCH.

However, more concerted efforts are necessary to stop the acid violence once and for all, he added.

Ronald W. Hiles, a plastic and reconstructive surgery consultant who has been visiting the country for the last 25 years and conducting plastic surgery free of charge, said, "Since 2002, the acid violence has reduced by 60 percent."

A Collective Effort Is Necessary to Stop Senseless Acid Abuse

Campaign against acid violence achieved significant success as it was handled from different angles, and the government, the NGOs and the media—all worked together to resist the violence, said Ronald noting that the violence is still taking place in the country.

"I think people who are throwing acid don't know what they are doing. They are doing it either from jealousy or from envy or greed. In developed countries, such types of violence are unusual and whenever I come across these acid victims, I become upset because it's not an accident, it's man-made and it shouldn't happen," Ronald added.

Referring to Nila's sufferings, Ronald said in an emotion-choked voice, "She had all her life before her, but that has changed now. One more acid violence is one too many and we want no more of it."

Indian Woman Protests Marriage Dowries

The Times of India

In the following viewpoint, a writer for The Times of India *discusses the protest of Pooja Chauhan, a twenty-two-year-old whose husband and husband's family mistreated her and demanded more dowry. The author reports on international and local reactions to what some have expressed to be an extreme protest. According to the author, Pooja walked the streets in her underwear to get the attention of police who had ignored her situation. The reporter points out that many argue that Pooja had no other choice but to protest in this manner, while others question her mental stability.* The Times of India *is a daily Indian newspaper.*

As you read, consider the following questions:

1. According to the author, the TimesofIndia.com poll said what percentage of people did not think Pooja's semi-nude protest was extreme?

2. According to the author, besides wanting more dowry, why was Pooja mistreated by her husband and in-laws?

3. According to the author, what does one person say a woman should not be seen as in terms of marriage?

When Pooja Chauhan stripped down to her underwear and walked the lanes of conservative Rajkot [India], she

The Times of India, "Pooja's Plight Evokes Strong Reactions," July 7, 2007. www.india times.com. Reproduced by permission.

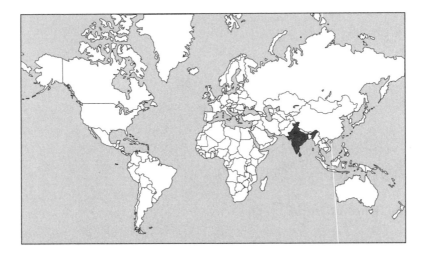

wanted to draw the attention of apathetic authorities. Little did she know that within the next 48 hours she would be known globally, symbolic of the thousands of Indian women who suffer the horrors that emanate from the greed of dowry-seekers.

Only unlike many other women, the 22-year-old decided to protest, stirring a storm in what was definitely larger than a tea cup. Letters of horror, of wonder, some queasy, some censorious are pouring in by the minute. Largely Indians, netizens [people who are citizens of online communities] from the world over are writing in to express their disgust at the treatment of women in Indian society.

The World Reacts to Pooja's Protest

On a TimesofIndia.com debate asking whether Pooja was victim or culprit, 82 percent of respondents wrote in favour of Pooja, hailing her as courageous and agreeing that the 22-year-old mother was a victim. But there was a not negligible 18 percent that felt she stepped the line by stepping out in public in her underwear.

Of these, most were people who sympathised with her, but thought the form of protest too extreme in the Indian context. Like Abhinav Chandra from Bangalore, who wrote that "The action was really extreme and the protest of such kinds may lead others to protest in this manner." Rave Kumar from Pune said that although the action she took was too extreme, "It seems she was left with no other option."

Or Lokesh Pathak from Delhi who says: "Pooja might be a victim, but behaving like this in society is certainly not acceptable. You cannot do just anything to draw your attention. This act should be condemned." Rishi from Boston agrees when he says: "It is ridiculous to brand her as a victim. Allegation of dowry is the fastest and surest way of getting back at the in-laws."

In fact, though an overwhelming number of people wrote words of sympathy and support for Pooja, when asked in the TimesofIndia.com poll—"Was the Rajkot resident's semi-nude protest too extreme?"—the ayes and nays were more even. For 40 percent of respondents to the poll said "Yes" it was. And 57 percent said "No" it wasn't. A small 3 percent did not wish to go either way.

"There is a law that protects the women from any sort of harassment and the police are to take immediate action."

The protestations come mostly from men readers, while women seem to feel a kinship with Pooja. And many men too.

The Police Ignored Pooja

Pooja has alleged that her husband and in-laws mistreated her and demanded more dowry. They also did not like the fact that she had bore a girl child. Debashis Bakshi from Patna strongly feels that "the husband and in-laws of this unfortunate woman should be punished so that no one can dare think of torturing women for dowry."

Hormaz Patel from Perth in Australia writes in to say, "Shame on the police and the society at large for pushing a

---

Mother-in-Law Dowry Abuse

The largest prison in Delhi, Tihar Jail, has a "mother-in-law" cell block, currently home to roughly 120 women, some of whom are serving 20-year sentences for murdering their daughters-in-law. The majority of these crimes stem from disputes over dowry: A bride whose dowry payments are viewed as inadequate is burned to death by her in-laws or husband, the cause of death listed as "kitchen accident." According to India's National Crime Record Bureau, one dowry death is reported every 77 minutes. The bureau recorded 7,026 dowry deaths in 2005 alone.

Abigail Lavin, "Dowry Disgrace: India's 'Kitchen Accident' Epidemic,"
The Weekly Standard, *November 29, 2006.*

---

person to such an extent. There is a law that protects the women from any sort of harassment and the police are to take immediate action. But I guess in a state like Gujarat, women are left to fend for themselves. Hang your heads in shame." Hormaz's outburst is echoed by many other readers. And the police are the target of much of the ire for its apathy in case, which readers say is what led to Pooja's unusual protest. Prashant from Pune feels that she "has a genuine reason behind this act and the police should have taken action."

From Singapore Rakesh Mahajan, says: "Our police have a very thick skin. They ignored Pooja earlier and hence she had to take such an extreme action. It's not her fault."

And Jaya, writing in from Bangalore, says: "Only Pooja must have known what she was going through, it's very easy to comment. If she has gone to such an extent it only shows how corrupt our society is. What Indian culture are we talking about when men in senior positions and authority cannot take care of a woman who is being ill treated?" And then the echo that resonates through the many letters of outrage: "Shame on us."

Sympathising with her plight, Vikram from Chandigarh writes: "Pooja took this measure so that her voice is heard and now it seems that the police have finally woken up and taken her in-laws into custody." The ordeal for Pooja is still not over as the police are planning to book her for 'indecent behaviour.'

Divided Opinions: Mentally Unstable or Brave?

Anil Desai, from Mumbai, however, feels differently. He poses: "I would rather ask people to check whether she is mentally sound to take such drastic step. I totally agree that we need to look beyond nudity. But was it really needed? What made her to take this extreme step?"

As though to counter his argument is one from Sanjay Kohli in London, who writes: "This is very similar to a scene in the movie *Lage Raho Munna Bhai* [translates to Carry On Munna Bhai] in which an old man removes most of his clothes to pay the bribe the official was demanding. The whole nation applauded the scene and appreciated the problem of bribery in our society. Therefore, Rajkot's semi-nude protest should be seen in the same perspective."

More Gandhigiri [identifies the ideals of Mahatma Ghandi, Indian political and spiritual leader]. Ajay Bhutani from Canada congratulates Pooja and states: "Sixty years of freedom, economic growth envied by the rest of the world, India shining, yet we torture our women for dowry and bearing daughters. I think Gandhi *ji* [Mahatma Ghandi] would have heartily endorsed this non-violent protest."

While the appropriateness of Pooja's protest is still being debated, there is aspect that has almost universal agreement. That a husband, who loved her and then married her, and the in-laws should be taken to task for driving Pooja to such extremes. Sajja from Uganda writes: "The husband and in-laws of this unfortunate woman should be punished so that no one can dare think of torturing women for dowry. My full sympathy is there with this unfortunate woman."

"A female is not a lottery ticket that you marry to win some money."

Tara Chopra writes from New York to say, "What was the Indian police doing all this time. Action should be taken against Pooja's despicable husband and in-laws as well as the police. Modi should make her the minister for women's welfare."

An emotional letter from Kiran Kumar, Jalandhar, who says evocatively: "A female is not a lottery ticket that you marry to win some money. We need to revere a lady. Stop this Durga Puja [biggest festival in Bengal, which celebrates Durga, the goddess of divine power] and Navratras [nine holy days dedicated to Durga] if we cannot respect the living Goddess."

But a reader Sanjay Pandita would rather not join the chorus. He asks why the in-laws and husband were arrested on the complaint of someone whose mental condition the same police are questioning. "The answer," he says, "lies in our laws such as 498A, the Domestic Violence Act and Dowry Act. When it comes to cases under these well-intentioned, but highly misused laws, the police, as a matter of rule, arrest without bothering to check out the bona fide of the complainant, as they did in this case. God save Indian Family!"

Indian Men Claim Misuse of the Dowry Act

Randeep Ramesh

In the following viewpoint, Randeep Ramesh reveals a male perspective of India's Dowry Act, which he argues makes husbands the victims in Indian marriages. According to Ramesh, some men claim that wives exploit the Act created to protect them from abuse and blackmail to gain money and legitimize divorce. He contends that a change in women's roles from housekeepers to career women is said to disagree with many Indian men who believe traditional marriage is disappearing. Thus, Ramesh concludes that tension is caused between women who refuse to take submissive roles and men who claim marriage has lost its identity. Ramesh is a foreign correspondent for The Guardian.

As you read, consider the following questions:

1. Under the anti-dowry law, how many people were arrested and how many were convicted by December of 2007, as cited by Ramesh?

2. In rebuke of Indian men who believe the Dowry Act should be relaxed, H.P.S. Virk, deputy commissioner of police, claims that what percentage of women exploit the act for their dishonest gain?

Randeep Ramesh, "Dowry Law Making Us the Victims, Says India's Men's Movement," *The Guardian* (London, England), December 13, 2007. www.guardian.co.uk. Copyright © 2007 Guardian News and Media Limited. Reproduced by permission of Guardian News Service, Ltd.-

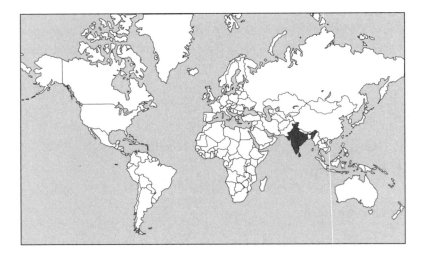

3. According to Ramesh, do more husbands or wives commit suicide in India? Approximately how many and for
what reasons stated?

Before the five armed police burst through Abhishek
Kumar's bedroom door in his Delhi apartment last summer, the software engineer had been prepared. His parents
had been moved out and a bag of his was packed for prison.
His crime, he explains, was a failed marriage.

Kumar's wife, Pratibha, a lecturer at a local college, had
made a complaint under India's dowry law. The offence would
allow for arrest and jailing of him and his parents without investigation.

The couple married in late 2005, but Pratibha left the
marital home after five days and the marriage was never con-
summated. Months later she claimed her husband had threatened to kill her if she did not produce a dowry that included
a hatchback car and 100,000 rupees (£1,250) in cash. He has
denied the allegations.

"I spent six weeks sharing a small prison cell with thieves
and murderers," said twenty-five-year-old Kumar, who was re-

leased on bail. "They had been convicted of a crime. I was innocent but was treated like a guilty man."

After he agreed to pay £8,750 in an out-of-court settlement, his wife withdrew the charges and the couple divorced this October.

"One men's organisation is demanding a ministry for men, arguing that 82% of taxpayers are men but that no money has ever been allocated for 'male welfare.'"

The cautionary tale appears to be part of a trend in middle-class India where male angst is on the rise. Men complain that they have lost their traditional role as providers as women work more. Further, women with independent incomes are refusing to submit to the traditional ideal of marriage where an obedient wife accedes to a husband's every wish.

The outcome is an undisguised backlash against Indian feminism and women's rights. One men's organisation is demanding a ministry for men, arguing that 82% of taxpayers are men but that no money has ever been allocated for "male welfare."

The protection enshrined in Indian law for harassed wives has also led to a deep-seated sense of male victimhood. The men's movement in the country has been fired up by what it claims is the "legal terrorism driven by radical groups . . . which has resulted in the blatant violation of men's rights."

Men's groups accept that Indian society has discriminated against women for centuries. But they say it is wrong to use legal measures to correct historical inequalities.

In India arranged marriages are still the norm and dowries are negotiated between families. In 1983 an anti-dowry act came into force to protect brides who were being attacked, and in some cases killed, by husbands trying to extort money from their families. Those found guilty face up to three years in jail. Up to the start of December this year [2007] Delhi police had registered 1,642 anti-dowry cases. However, the men's movement says the law is being "misused" by wives. Unscrupulous women, they say, see the law as a tool to extract as much money as possible from their partners.

Every Saturday in Delhi a group of young professional men gathers to share experiences. They counsel each other over the trauma of "systematic abuse by wives."

Swarup Sarkar, of the Save Indian Family Foundation, which has 8,000 members in Delhi alone, said: "Women protection laws assume that women are always honest and truthful. Therefore, proof and evidence is not required. So honest men are being jailed. Men are committing suicide. It has become an instrument not of equality but terror."

At the men's meetings, lawyers dispense free advice and their nervous clients finger leaflets explaining the "ugly reality of dowry law."

Sarkar, who works in marketing, set up the foundation after his wife filed a "false case" against him in 2002. "I know what it is like not to be able to sleep or work. We want only gender-neutral laws not one-sided ones."

He talks of government data which show that 134,757 people were arrested under the anti-dowry law but only 5,739 people were convicted. He wants the anti-dowry offence decriminalised and the threat of jail removed. The change, say police and women's groups, would mean fewer women coming forward.

"This misuse business really is complete rubbish," said Indira Jaisingh, a supreme court lawyer, who successfully lobbied last year for a new domestic violence act in India. "From a low conviction rate, you cannot conclude a law is wrong. Just look at conviction rates for rape in England which are also low but nobody says rape does not happen."

Jaisingh said that since Indian women still lived in joint family households, an anti-dowry law would need to protect

Anti-Dowry Laws Draw Protest in India

Protesters have in recent months taken to the streets under banners bearing slogans such as "Stop legal terrorism!", referring to how some Indian women abuse anti-dowry laws by falsely accusing their husbands and families of vindictiveness, and "Stop husband suicides!", seeking to draw attention to the innocent men who have taken their lives after being thrown into jail on such charges.

Spearheading the movement against the anti-dowry law is the Save Indian Family Foundation, set up in the capital two years ago. Its members number about 10,000 in nine cities and it has called for the establishment of a "men's ministry" to protect the interests of India's men.

Amrit Dhillon,
"Wives Show Their Clause,"
South China Morning Post, *January 10, 2008.*

wives from a husband and his family seeking money. "The jail option is there because of the violence used by members of the joint family. We probably need more laws for women to ensure, for example, equitable distribution of property on divorce."

At the headquarters of Delhi's crime against women unit, set up to investigate "marriage abuses", police meet the claims of "male victims" with scepticism. H.P.S. Virk, the deputy commissioner of police and head of the unit, said a "small minority of women misuse the law." Adding, "In my experience, it would be just 2% of cases."

The problem was that of new money alongside old mindsets.

The booming economy has raised the price of wedlock, a ritual still governed by the past. In Indian weddings there is widespread acceptance of the inequality between bride givers and bride takers. The bride's family, according to convention, gives to, but never takes, from the groom's family. In today's India that tends to translate into ever more expensive dowries.

"In the merchant class we are seeing open auctions of marriageable men. If your son has a shop in a good location, the bride will have to pay 10m rupees [£125,000]," said Virk. "Until such mindsets change, and that will not be for a long time, I cannot see how women need less protection."

Explainer: Gender War

The first shots have been fired in India's gender war. There are about 60 Web sites committed to promoting the well-being of men in India. Men's groups say males are increasingly subject to myriad forms of subtle discrimination in the name of progress.

"Police say that every 33 minutes a crime is committed against a woman in India and there is one 'dowry death' in the country every 104 minutes."

Some groups cite job insecurity and unemployment as the problem. In the five years to 2005, 1.4 million men lost their jobs while one million women gained new employment.

On crime, too, the men's movement is sifting through official statistics to counter claims that women in India bear the brunt of violence—though police say that every 33 minutes a crime is committed against a woman in India and there is one "dowry death" in the country every 104 minutes.

The Save Indian Family Foundation argues that, compared with women, nearly twice as many married men (up to 52,483) take their own lives—being "unable to withstand verbal, emotional, economic and physical abuse."

But on social indicators Indian women are clearly far behind men. Less than half of the women in India can read or write, compared with 75% of men. In the past 20 years more than 10 million female fetuses have been aborted.

The male lobby claimed a symbolic victory when the government of India observed an international men's day in November.

Filipino Mail-Order Brides Are in Danger of Abusive Marriages

Shay Cullen

In the following viewpoint, Shay Cullen argues that the mail-order bride industry is dangerous, focusing on trafficked Filipino women. Cullen addresses the violence and lack of love in the marriages into which these women are sold. Shay Cullen, a Columbian missionary working in the Philippines since 1969, writes for Women in Action, *a magazine that reports on women's issues on a global scale.*

As you read, consider the following questions:

1. According to Cullen, what percentage of the thirty-five thousand trafficked Filipino women go to Japan?
2. According to Cullen, what percentage of Thai and Filipino mail-order brides who wed in Japan learn to speak Japanese?
3. According to the author, what is the estimated number of "bogus" marriages arranged in the Netherlands in the early 1990s?

The 'mail-order bride' industry is a cold and callous trade. If you are in any doubt about that, you need only click on the Internet and wonder at the name of one particular service

Shay Cullen, "The Miserable Lives of Mail-Order Brides," *Women in Action*, vol. 3, December 2002, p. 6. Copyright © 2002 Isis International. Reproduced by permission.

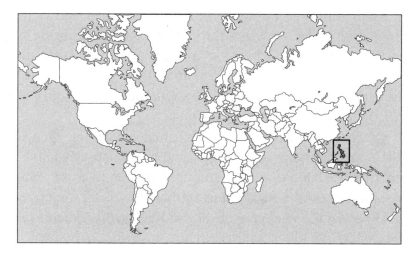

offering 'marriage-minded Filipinos' the "Mail Order Bride Warehouse." Heartless businesses such as this have been occupying human rights campaigners for decades, but progress against their activities has been limited. In fact, their trade is booming.

Every year, tens of thousands of young girls and women are packed off to the West under the pretence that they will be entering into a rewarding marriage and a new life of prosperity. Nowadays a huge number come not just from South East Asia but also from Russia and Eastern European countries. Often, the women are trapped in actual or virtual slavery, or in rings of prostitution.

The Unethical and Inhumane Business of Trafficking Women

Some 50,000 women are lured to the United States alone every year, but 90 percent of the 35,000 trafficked women who leave the Philippines each year go to Japan. "There they find themselves sold on as brides or as 'entertainers,' or as victims of the 'Vaginal Economy,'" in the sad words of one women's rights campaigner in Manila.

Many trafficked women, and even girls, are indeed victims of fraud and fake marriages through the mail-order bride system. They end up in loveless marriages, in forced prostitution and repressive labour. Others are almost enslaved by uncaring husbands who deprive them of personal freedom, money and civil rights, and use them as sex objects.

Of course there are many legitimate marriage agencies. There are traditions of arranged marriages between families, and 'matchmaking'—a long honoured custom in many societies—that cannot be regarded as trafficking.

However, the marrying off of children aged between twelve and sixteen to older adult men for a dowry, as happens in parts of Africa and the Middle East, is another matter. Some may see this as legitimate, but in reality, it is a form of sexual exploitation of children.

But there are many thousands of normal encounters between western men and women from poor developing countries that result in good, happy marriages. What concerns campaigners and authorities worldwide is the growing practice of treating young women as commodities to be bought and sold in a web of exploitation and enslavement.

The Horrors Faced by Filipino Mail-Order Brides

In Japan, Thai or Filipino brides are married to farmers and lead lives of boredom, docility and dependency, devoid of meaningful communication. Fewer than 10 percent learn fluent Japanese.

In Australia, several Filipino women have been brutally assaulted or murdered in remote sheep stations where they were brought in as wives. Despite the horror stories, the casual visitor to the Australian Embassy in Manila still sees queues of beer-bellied husbands-to-be in their 60s with their prospective brides applying for a spousal visa. "It won't happen to me," the women think, and they are usually right. The violent

Cambodian Bride Trafficking Is a Growing Trend for South Korean Men

Operating in a shadowy legal space, questions have been raised about the possible exploitative nature of [international marriage brokers who run "matchmaking" services for men seeking Cambodian brides], which some contend [have] acted as a front for global human trafficking rings. . . .

South Koreans make up a large percentage of the men seeking brides in Cambodia. In 2005, marriages to foreigners accounted for 14% of all marriages in South Korea, up from 4% in 2000. According to the United States 2007 Trafficking in Persons Report, 72% of South Korean men in foreign marriages marry women from Southeast Asia or Mongolia. They are often lured by billboards which dot the South Korean countryside, advertising marriage services to foreigners. . . .

Marriages between Cambodian women and South Korean men are known to be fraught with difficulties, frequently caused by huge cultural and linguistic divides. "Often the women have misguided expectations of what life may be like abroad; there is a lack of realistic information about life in Korea," the IOM's [International Organization for Migration] report says.

Brian McCartan, "Not All Bliss for Take-Away Cambodian Brides,"
Asia Times, *April 8, 2008.*

deaths and spousal abuse may be rare, but the long servitude to a loveless marriage is almost certainly something that will be happening to them.

Young women are frequently duped into believing that by marrying a foreigner, they will be rich and thus escape grinding poverty and unemployment. They do it to help their families, but it seldom works out as hoped.

For many, it is a form of modern-day slavery, replacing the "bonded servitude" of the past. "The person may enter into an agreement with the recruiting agent on an apparently voluntary basis but conditions at the destination point are likely to involve coercion, including physical abuse, restrictions on freedom of movement, abuse and violence, and fraud," says a recent 128-page study from the International Labour Organisation.

"'The men there (in Europe) think we Filipinos are docile and submissive and that they can treat us like domestic servants, but they are wrong; we know our rights and dignity,' said Josie, a former mail-order bride who divorced an abusive husband she met through the Internet."

In the early 1990s, as many as 5,000 bogus marriages were being arranged in the Netherlands annually. Following media exposure of mail-order bride traffic, authorities stopped the practice.

"The men there (in Europe) think we Filipinos are docile and submissive and that they can treat us like domestic servants, but they are wrong; we know our rights and dignity," said Josie, a former mail-order bride who divorced an abusive husband she met through the Internet.

German Judge Cites Koran to Justify Abuse in Moroccan Couple's Divorce Case

Veit Medick and Anna Reimann

In the following viewpoint, Veit Medick and Anna Reimann report on a Moroccan couple's divorce case in which a German judge referred to the Koran, the central religious text for Muslims, to excuse the husband's abuse toward his wife. The authors argue that the passage from the Koran that the judge cited is controversial among Muslims because it may or may not be interpreted as an allowance for a husband to beat his wife. Medick and Reimann are reporters for Spiegel, *a weekly magazine published in Hamburg, Germany.*

As you read, consider the following questions:

1. According to Medick and Reimann, under what description did the Moroccan wife and her lawyer file her divorce to qualify for an immediate divorce?

2. According to the authors, what is the phrase used by the judge that has been interpreted to mean that a "husband can beat his wife"?

3. According to the authors, what is the reply the judge sent to the Moroccan wife's lawyer in response to being asked to step down from the case due to a "conflict of interest"?

Veit Medick and Anna Reimann, "A German Judge Cites Koran in Divorce Case," *Spiegel Online*, March 21, 2007. www.spiegel.de. Copyright © 2007 Spiegel Online. Reproduced by permission.

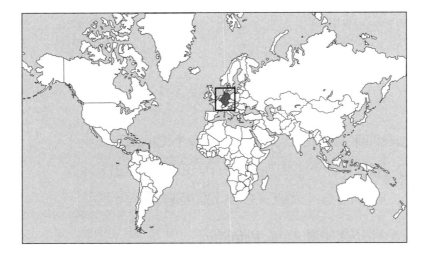

The case seems simply too strange to be true. A twenty-six -year-old mother of two wanted to free herself from what had become a miserable and abusive marriage. The police had even been called to their apartment to separate the two—both of Moroccan origin—after her husband got violent in May 2006. The husband was forced to move out, but the terror continued: Even after they separated, the spurned husband threatened to kill his wife.

A quick divorce seemed to be the only solution—the twenty-six-year-old was unwilling to wait the year between separation and divorce mandated by German law. She hoped that as soon as they were no longer married, her husband would leave her alone. Her lawyer, Barbara Becker-Rojczyk agreed and she filed for immediate divorce with a Frankfurt court last October. They both felt that the domestic violence and death threats easily fulfilled the "hardship" criteria necessary for such an accelerated split.

In January, though, a letter arrived from the judge adjudicating the case. The judge rejected the application for a speedy divorce by referring to a passage in the Koran that some have controversially interpreted to mean that a husband can beat his wife. It's a supposed right which is the subject of intense debate among Muslim scholars and clerics alike. "The exercise of the right to castigate does not fulfill the hardship criteria as defined by Paragraph 1565 (of German federal law)," the daily *Frankfurter Rundschau* [newspaper printed in Frankfurt, Germany] quoted the judge's letter as saying. It must be taken into account, the judge argued, that both man and wife have Moroccan backgrounds.

"The Husband Can Beat His Wife"

"The right to castigate means for me: the husband can beat his wife," Becker-Rojczyk said, interpreting the judge's verdict.

In an interview with Spiegel Online, Becker-Rojczyk said the judge indicated to her that it makes no sense to insist on an accelerated divorce. The judge's advice? Wait for the year-long waiting period to elapse.

The lawyer and her client were shocked. Immediately, they filed a claim alleging that the judge should have recused herself due to a conflict of interest. They felt that, because of the point of view presented by the judge, she was unable to reach an objective verdict. In the reply sent to Becker-Rojczyk, the judge expressly referred to a Koran verse—or sura—which indicates that a man's honor is injured when his wife behaves in an unchaste manner. "Apparently the judge deems it unchaste when my client adapts a Western lifestyle," Becker-Rojczyk said.

On Tuesday evening, Becker-Rojczyk expressed amazement that the judge was still on the bench, given that the controversial verdict was handed down weeks ago. Becker-Rojczyk had elected to go public with the case to attract attention to the judge's conduct. It seems to have worked. On Wednesday, after the Tuesday evening publication of the story on Spiegel Online, the attorney received a fax from the Frankfurt court granting the conflict of interest claim and excusing the judge from the case.

Passage of the Koran Sometimes Interpreted as an Allowance for a Husband to Beat His Wife

Men are the maintainers of women because Allah has made some of them to excel others and because they spend out of their property; the good women are therefore obedient, guarding the unseen as Allah has guarded; and (as to) those on whose part you fear desertion, admonish them, and leave them alone in the sleeping-places and beat them; then if they obey you, do not seek a way against them; surely Allah is High, Great.

The Koran, 4:34. http://quod.lib.umich.edu.

Still, it is unlikely that the case will be heard again before the mandated year of separation expires in May. But the judge who heard the case may have to face further consequences for her decision. On Wednesday, numerous politicians in Berlin voiced their horror at the verdict—and demanded disciplinary action against the judge.

"In cases of marital violence, there have been a number of cases where the perpetrator's culture of origin has been considered as a mitigating circumstance."

Further Investigation

"In my opinion, this is a case of extreme violation of the rule of law that can't be solved with a mere conflict of interest ruling," Social Democrat parliamentarian Dieter Wiefelspütz told Spiegel Online. "There have to be further consequences. This is a case for judicial supervision—this case needs to be further investigated."

The deputy floor leader for the Christian Democrats, Wolfgang Bosbach, agreed. "This is a sad example of how the conception of the law from another legal and cultural environment is taken as the basis for our own notion of law," he said on Wednesday.

This isn't the first time that German courts have used cultural background to inform their verdicts. Christa Stolle of the women's rights organization Terre des Femmes said that in cases of marital violence, there have been a number of cases where the perpetrator's culture of origin has been considered as a mitigating circumstance—although such verdicts have become seldom in recent years.

But there remains quite a bit of work to do. "In my work educating sexist and short-sighted Muslim men," asked Michaela Sulaika Kaiser of the Network for Muslim Women, "do I now have to convince German courts that women are also people on the same level with men and that they, like any other human, have the right to be protected from physical and psychological violence?"

Periodical Bibliography

The following articles have been selected to supplement the diverse views presented in this chapter.

Arusha Times	"Tanzania; Human Rights," December 8, 2007.
Kelvin Chan	"Forced-Marriage Debate Lifts Veil on Vows Built on Violence," *South China Morning Post*, July 3, 2006.
Park Chung-a	"Marriage Agencies Violate Women's Rights," *Korea Times*, November 13, 2006.
International Humanist and Ethical Union	"Child Marriage: A Violation of Human Rights," April 23, 2007. www.iheu.org.
Korea Times	"Abuse of Vietnamese Wives," November 2, 2007.
The Monitor	"Uganda; To Marry or Not to Marry From Your Clan; That is the Question," July 2, 2006.
New Straits Times (Malaysia)	"Mail-Order Brides," August 20, 2006.
Teddy Ng	"Abuse Plagues Cross-Border Marriages," *ChinaDaily.com.cn*, May 10, 2007. www.chinadaily.com.
Justin Norrie	"Behind Closed Doors, the Violence Continues; Japan," *Sydney Morning Herald*, March 22, 2008.
Leigh Pasqual	"Rape is Rape, No Excuses Please," *The Straits Times* (Singapore), November 27, 2006.
James Slack	"Forced Marriage Is an Intolerable Abuse, Says Judge," *Daily Mail* (London), July 6, 2006.
Sunita Thakur	"India's Acid Victims Demand Justice," *BBC News*, April 9, 2008.
UN Integrated Regional Information Networks	"Niger; Where Childhood Ends On the Marriage Bed," December 19, 2007.

GLOBALVIEWPOINTS

CHAPTER 2

Arranged Marriage, Child Marriage, and Polygamy

Marriages Arranged by Class Are Antiquated

Christina Patterson

In the following viewpoint, Christina Patterson argues that arranged marriages based on class are coupling people who are too similar. Patterson describes different ways people today are being matched within categories such as education and background. Patterson is an associate editor of and contributor to The Independent's *comment desk since 2007, and formerly served as a literary editor for the newspaper. She reports on books, politics, the arts, and cultural issues.*

As you read, consider the following questions:

1. According to Patterson, what was the method of arranging marriages that she witnessed while in Shanghai?

2. According to Patterson, when arranged marriages are not successful and violence ensues, what is the term used to explain the killing of a family member?

3. In referring to Shakespeare, what word does Patterson use to describe class-based arranged marriage to support her opinion?

In his Booker-of-Bookers-winning novel, *Midnight's Children*, Salman Rushdie (or Sir Salman, as we must now call

Christina Patterson, "Class: It's the Key to Arranged Marriages," *The Independent* (London, England), November 2, 2007, p. 44. Copyright © 2007 Independent Newspapers (UK) Ltd. Reproduced by permission.

him) gives a description of an arranged marriage which would warm the cockles of the heart of the most hide-bound Muslim matriarch.

"Each day," says Rushdie of his character, Amina, "she selected one fragment of Ahmed Sinai, and concentrated her entire being upon it until it became wholly familiar; until she felt fondness rising up within her and becoming affection and, finally, love." She does this because she has "resolved to fall in love with her husband bit by bit". Luckily, it works.

It's a model for romance which has filtered down the centuries. Where the head leads, the heart (surely) follows. It's a model which has kept kingdoms, alliances and political dynasties intact, and one of which vast swathes of the world's current population are the product.

"'My approach to arranged marriages,' says Aneela Rahman, presenter of Arrange Me a Marriage, *who will practise on live, human guinea pigs, 'is pragmatic, focusing on compatibility—looking at shared goals, background, values, education, earning potential.'"*

Arranged Marriages Based on Class

In Shanghai last week [November 2007], I emerged from an almost scarily high-tech digital art exhibition in a gallery in the People's Park to find swarms of middle-aged men and women staring at bits of paper on the bushes. Was it, I wondered, a sale of calligraphy? Or some kind of public art? My Chinese guide giggled. "Oh no," she said, "it's lonely hearts."

Lonely hearts for the middle-aged, and in such a public place! How sweet, I gushed, that they were so unembarrassed. My guide's smile twitched into an expression of pure horror. "No!" she shrieked. "It is for their children!" The scripts laid out so carefully on the bushes were their children's CVs [curriculum vitae or resume]. Degrees in one corner of the park, MAs in another, and PhDs in another.

Inter-Caste Marriage Is Risky in India

The most vehement opposition in India is to inter-caste marriages. . . . [In a 2007 opinion poll of 15,000 people], three-quarters of Indians said it was wrong to marry a person from a different caste. India remains a stratified society and the caste system relies on marriages being arranged to preserve bloodlines and lineage. A romance across the caste divide is often fatal. In the back streets of a poor housing colony in east Delhi, a father weeps for his dead son. Chander Bhan Kumar, who comes from a dalit, or untouchable, community, says his eldest boy, Kishan, was killed because he dared to marry an upper-caste girl, Laxmi, in 2005.

Randeep Ramesh, "India: Modernizing Fast—
But Beware if You Try to Choose Who to Marry:
Love Stories Highlight Durability of Class and Religious Divides,"
The Guardian, *April 9, 2007.*

In the past few decades, arranged marriages have once again become a feature of British life, as Pakistani, Indian and Bangladeshi immigrants have imported the traditions they've grown up with. As in so many other culturally "challenging" areas, the British response has been confused. North Londoners, whose sexual freedom has led to domestic arrangements that can only be described as complicated, will tell you earnestly that arranged marriages are often very "successful". Casualties, when it all goes horribly wrong, are referred to as victims not of murder, but of "honour killings" [murder committed by members of a family against a female member of the family said to have brought dishonor upon the family]. Look how tolerant we are! And did you know that our national dish is chicken tikka masala?

Television Meets Tradition

The latest institution to fall for this nonsense, is, predictably enough, the BBC [British Broadcasting Company]. In its tireless quest for ratings, punctuated with the odd effort to ensure that black and Asian faces are occasionally tolerated outside the canteen, it has hit on a sure-fire formula: A reality-TV show presented by a photogenic young British Pakistani woman, which aims to combine the contemporary obsession with dating with the traditional principles of an Asian arranged marriage.

"My approach to arranging marriages," says Aneela Rahman, presenter of *Arrange Me A Marriage*, who will practise on live, human guinea pigs, "is pragmatic, focusing on compatibility—looking at shared goals, background, values, education, earning potential".

Lexi Proud, the guinea pig who features in the first programme, and who is shamefully single at 33, has been unsuccessful, Rahman says, because she has dated people "outside her class".

Quite right, too. Obviously, what we need in the twenty-first century, in a multicultural society, are clearer demarcations of culture and class. Stick with your own. Don't get ideas above—or below—your station. Homogeneity, to paraphrase Shakespeare, is all. Arrange me a marriage, yes—but first, find me a clone.

Some Bangladeshi Girls Are Challenging the Tradition of Child Marriages

Steve Nettleton

In the following viewpoint, Steve Nettleton argues the importance of a UNICEF-supported program called Kishori Abhijan, or "adolescent's journey," which teaches girls that they have a right to refuse marriage at a young age, while helping to educate them about decision making in terms of business and life in general. Nettleton reinforces the need for such a program by pointing out that half of all Bangladeshi girls are married by age fifteen. Nettleton is a correspondent for UNICEF, the United Nations Children's Fund, which addresses such issues as the recognition of children's rights and the need to empower girls through education.

As you read, consider the following questions:

1. According to Nettleton, what is the legal age for marriage in Bangladesh?

2. According to the author, what percentage of Bangladeshi girls are mothers by the time they are nineteen years old?

3. How does Mosamad Rina Akhter respond to parents who worry that if their daughters wait to marry they may be less secure?

Steve Nettleton, "Empowering Girls by Challenging the Tradition of Child Marriage," UNICEF, August 23, 2006. Reproduced by permission.

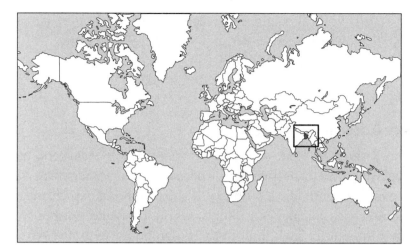

Less than a year ago, Mosamad Mounjera Khatun watched as her future was decided without her consent. Her parents had arranged for her to be married, though she was only 14 years old. Like most young brides, she would have been forced to drop out of school and work in her in-laws' household.

"About half of all girls [in Bangladesh] are married by the age of 15."

"I wore a sullen face," said Mosamad. "My friends asked me why I looked so unhappy. I told them that I want to get on with my studies but my parents want me to get married. But I do not want to get married now."

Child marriage is a common plight in Bangladesh. The legal age for marriage is 18 for girls, and 21 for boys. However, about half of all girls are married by the age of fifteen, and 60 percent become mothers by the age of nineteen. Early pregnancy and childbirth often lead to health complications. An estimated 50 percent of adolescent girls are undernourished and suffer from anemia. Most are not properly educated about reproductive health and contraception, and are often vulnerable to dowry-related violence, kidnappings and rape.

A [United Nations Children's Fund] UNICEF-supported program is working to give these girls a say in their own future.

An Adolescent's Journey

The Kishori Abhijan project aims to empower teenagers, particularly girls, to participate in decisions about their lives and become role models for others. Kishori Abhijan, which means "adolescent's journey" in Bangla, works to create a supportive environment for girls in both their own households and within the community.

The project focuses on providing leadership skills and life skills for unmarried girls on issues such as child marriage, reproductive health and HIV/AIDS. It also offers technical training for livelihoods such as garment production or photography, as well as advice on how to start a business.

It is hoped that girls will gain the self-esteem and confidence to take control of their lives.

"We feel that if the adolescent boys and girls can take care of themselves, then that is a step forward, at least for them," said Rosy Parvin, a unit organizer for the Kishori Abhijan project in Chapai Nawabganj, near the western Bangladeshi city of Rajshahi. "In the past, a village girl did not have any right to talk about herself. Today, she can talk with her parents and also negotiate with them. She can say if they are doing something wrong."

A Better Future for the Whole Family

With help from her friends in the project, Mosamad broke off her pending marriage. Peer counsellor Mosamad Rina Akhter and other members appealed to the girl's parents to cancel the wedding.

At first, the parents resisted. They believed if they waited, it would be difficult to arrange a marriage for her.

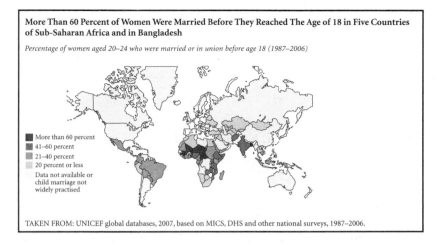

More Than 60 Percent of Women Were Married Before They Reached The Age of 18 in Five Countries of Sub-Saharan Africa and in Bangladesh

Percentage of women aged 20–24 who were married or in union before age 18 (1987–2006)

■ More than 60 percent
■ 41–60 percent
▨ 21–40 percent
□ 20 percent or less
□ Data not available or
child marriage not
widely practised

TAKEN FROM: UNICEF global databases, 2007, based on MICS, DHS and other national surveys, 1987–2006.

"But we told them that if their daughter studies and becomes educated, then she would find a job for herself," said Ms. Akhter. "That way her future would be better, and at the same time, your future would be better too."

Thanks to that intervention, Mosamad remains single, and in school. She says she will decide her own career and will wait to get married, at a time of her own choosing.

Kishori Abhijan's Rosy Parvin said it is one success story which can lead to many more.

"If I can stop the system of dowry or early marriage, then those girls will be automatically empowered," said Ms. Parvin. "Girls will know that no one can force them into marriage before they turn 18."

American Youth in Utah Defend Polygamy

Jennifer Dobner

In the following viewpoint, Jennifer Dobner argues that while Utah's constitution prohibits plural marriages, a handful of Salt Lake City's youth rallied for the state's laws to change, stating that polygamy existed in Utah before it officially became a state. According to Dobner, a pro-polygamy education and advocacy group sponsored the rally, during which children and teens asked people to consider their rights to protect both their religious and nonreligious polygamist beliefs. Dobner is a staff writer for De-seret News, Utah's oldest newspaper.

As you read, consider the following questions:

1. According to Dobner, when did the members of The Church of Jesus Christ of Latter-day Saints first bring the practice of polygamy to Utah?

2. According to the author, what are some stereotypes of children of polygamist parents?

3. According to the author, how is polygamy treated under the Utah Constitution?

Calling their lives blessed, more than a dozen children and young adults from Utah polygamist families spoke at a rally Saturday [August 2006], calling for a change in state laws and the right to live the life and religion they choose.

Jennifer Dobner, "Youths Defend Plural Marriage," *Deseret News*, August 20, 2006. www.deseretnews.com. Copyright © 2006 The Deseret News Publishing Company. Reproduced by permission of Associated Press.

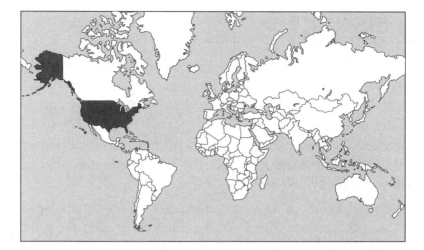

"Because of our beliefs, many of our people have been incarcerated and had their basic human rights stripped of them," said a 19-year-old identified only as Tyler. "Namely life, liberty and the pursuit of happiness. I didn't come here today to ask for your permission to live my beliefs. I shouldn't have to."

Pro-Polygamy Education

The youths, ages 10–20, belong to various religious sects, including Apostolic United Brethren, the Davis County Cooperative Society and Centennial Park, as well as families that practice polygamy independent of religious affiliation. They spoke voluntarily but gave only their first names, saying later they were protecting the privacy of their parents.

The rally, which drew a crowd of about 250 to Salt Lake's City Hall, is thought to be the first of its kind, said Mary Batchelor, cofounder of Principle Voices of Polygamy, a pro-polygamy education and advocacy group that helped organize the event.

Polygamy has been practiced here longer than Utah has been a state. First brought to the high desert by members of The Church of Jesus Christ of Latter-day Saints in 1846, the practice was abandoned by the church in 1890 as a condition of statehood, which was granted six years later.

The church now excommunicates members found to be practicing plural marriage.

Polygamy is banned in the Utah Constitution and is a felony offense under the state's bigamy statute. Those who choose to live "the principle," as it is known to insiders, typically try to live their lives secretly out of fear that attention will bring police to their door.

Rachel Young, a 45-year-old mother of one of the speakers, said that underlying fear kept some away from the rally.

"People are actually really scared to be known as polygamist because of the prejudice the public—not just the government—has about them," Young said.

Twenty-First Century Children of Polygamist Parents

Also absent Saturday were the stereotypes most often seen on television and in movies about polygamists and their kids— girls in prairie dresses with long, braided hair and boys in buttoned-to-the-collar long-sleeved shirts sporting dour expressions.

"'We are not brainwashed, mistreated, neglected, malnourished, illiterate, defective or dysfunctional,' 17-year-old Jessica said. 'My brothers and sisters are freethinking, independent people. Some who have chosen this lifestyle, while others have branched out to a diversity of religions.'"

Instead the kids here looked like any other teens. Dressed in flip-flops and blue jeans, bangs drooping over their eyes, they talked on cell phones and played rock music, crooning lyrics written to defend their family life.

Utah's State Constitution Prohibits Polygamy

Article 3 Section

The following ordinance shall be irrevocable without the consent of the United States and the people of this State: [Religious toleration—Polygamy forbidden.] First:—Perfect toleration of religious sentiment is guaranteed. No inhabitant of this State shall ever be molested in person or property on account of his or her mode of religious worship; but polygamous or plural marriages are forever prohibited.

Article XXIV, Section 2.

All laws of the Territory of Utah now in force, not repugnant to this Constitution, shall remain in force until they expire by their own limitations, or are altered or repealed by the Legislature. The act of the Governor and Legislative Assembly of the Territory of Utah, entitled, "An Act to punish polygamy and other kindred offenses," approved February 4th, A.D. 1892, in so far as the same defines and imposes penalties for polygamy, is hereby declared to be in force in the State of Utah.

Utah State Code

76-7-101. Bigamy—Defense.

1. A person is guilty of bigamy when, knowing he has a husband or wife or knowing the other person has a husband or wife, the person purports to marry another person or cohabits with another person.

2. Bigamy is a felony of the third degree.

3. It shall be a defense to bigamy that the accused reasonably believed he and the other person were legally eligible to remarry.

Tapestry Against Polygamy,
"Polygamy Background Information,"
April 30, 2008. www.polygamy.org.

All of the speakers praised their parents and families and said their lives were absent of the abuse, neglect, forced marriages and other "horror stories" sometimes associated with polygamist communities, particularly, the embattled southern Utah-based Fundamentalist Church of Jesus Christ of Latter-day Saints.

"We are not brainwashed, mistreated, neglected, malnourished, illiterate, defective or dysfunctional," 17-year-old Jessica said. "My brothers and sisters are freethinking, independent people. Some who have chosen this lifestyle, while others have branched out to a diversity of religions."

The youths, who called for an end to prejudice, were praised by organizers for their courage.

"You have paved the way for others to come forward as well," said Laura Fuller, a law student said to be a wife of well-known Utah polygamist John Daniel Kingston. "Today is just the first step. With courage like yours, someday, we will have the same rights as everyone else . . . someday we will have the freedom to live our religion."

Australian Bush Marriages of Children Are Recognized in the Community

Simon Kearney

In the following viewpoint, Simon Kearney argues that bush marriages of children in the Northern Territory of Australia are without ceremony; children simply say that they are married and the community recognizes them as husband and wife. Kearney points out that these marriages of children as young as thirteen years old often lead to very young mothers and quick-dissolving marriages. Kearney writes that some women in the community, who know the dangers of sexually transmitted diseases (STDs) and youth pregnancy, are warning girls of what might be a potential mistake. Kearney reports for The Australian.

As you read, consider the following questions:

1. According to Kearney, what was the average age of a first-time mother in Yuendumu from 2005–2007?

2. According to the author, what reason does Ms. Dickson give for young girls participating in bush marriages?

3. According to the author, how do Northern Territory police describe the behavior of children in Aboriginal communities in the Territory?

Simon Kearney, "Elders Alert to Bush Marriage," *The Australian*, August 7, 2007. Copyright © 2007 News Limited. Reproduced by permission of the publisher and the author.

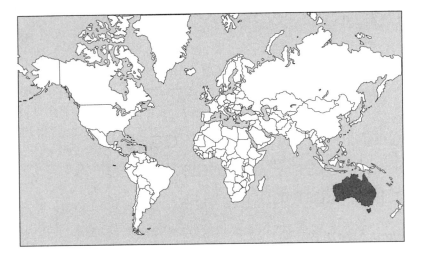

Belle Nakamarra Dickson runs a sexual education program at the Yuendumu Women's Centre [in Australia] titled "Strong women, strong children, strong culture".

Every week, she and the other grandmothers and aunties get into the women's night patrol troop carrier and cruise the town to pick up the young girls they have decided to target that week.

The 67-year-old has good reason to care as she has watched two of her granddaughters enter into bush marriages and have children, one at 14 and the other at 15.

> *"The birth records at the local health clinic show that the average age of a first-time mother . . . has been 15 for the past two years."*

Informal bush marriages are common in Yuendumu [a town in the Northern Territory of Australia]. Pam Malden, the coordinator of the women's centre, told *The Australian* children as young as 13 were living as man and wife in a family home and many of the town's children had already become sexually active at that age.

Ms Malden said bush marriages were culturally recognised in Yuendumu and many other communities. She said there was no ceremony—the couple simply declared themselves to be married and the union was recognised by the rest of the community.

The birth records at the local health clinic show that the average age of a first-time mother in the town, 300 km northwest of Alice Springs, has been 15 for the past two years.

Ms Dickson's granddaughter Bernadine Napangardi Watson is now 16; two months ago, she gave birth to a daughter, Chelsea Margaret Watson. The father is now 17 and the two are no longer together. "I don't like him any more," she said.

Ms Watson said lots of her school friends had had children in the town, as well.

Ms Dickson said young motherhood was all too common and about half of the "marriages" that led to the pregnancies were over very quickly. Many others were forced to stay together because their families felt shame about the age of the couple.

"Lots of young people, they're all having babies," she said.

Ms Dickson said it was generally thought of by young girls as a way of getting out of school or snaring a sought-after boy.

The Yuendumu School has nearly enough young mothers to qualify for funding for a creche [day care]. They fell one short last year.

It is frustrating for Ms Dickson to watch. Her fire-and-brimstone lectures on family planning often go unheard. "They're mad. I can't stop it. They don't listen," she said.

At home, Ms Dickson still has some influence, and Ms Watson has gone back to school at her grandmother's insistence.

Ms Malden said incidences of sexually transmitted diseases were relatively common among teenagers in the community.

Bush Marriages Are Common in Australia's Northern Territory

Informal bush marriages are common in Yuendumu, 300 km northwest of Alice Springs in the Northern Territory of Australia

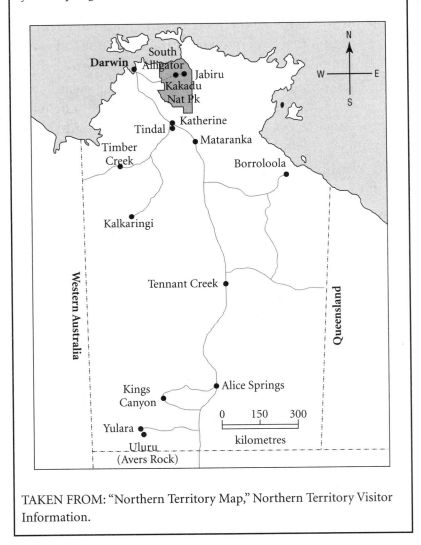

TAKEN FROM: "Northern Territory Map," Northern Territory Visitor Information.

Northern Territory police investigating child sexual abuse in Aboriginal communities in the Territory describe sexual behaviour among such young children as "sexualised behaviour" and it only serves to complicate the difficulty of their investigations.

They have several current cases involving dozens of sexually active children in remote communities that have pointed back to child sexual abuse by adults.

Yuendumu Council chairman Harry Nelson said child abuse had been occurring for years in Aboriginal communities and he complained it was disappointing that the Territory and federal governments had only acted in strength recently. But Mr Nelson said such abuse was not tolerated in the strong Warlpiri [a group of indigenous Australians] community of Yuendumu.

Some Chinese Parents Arrange Afterlife Marriages

Jim Yardley

In the following viewpoint, Jim Yardley argues that Chinese afterlife marriages are commonplace along the Yellow River in the Loess Plateau and extend from ancestor worship and a belief that "an unmarried life is incomplete." In afterlife marriages, the parents of a deceased bachelor son seek a dead single woman to be buried beside him. Yardley points out that it is common for parents to pay approximately four years of income to make sure their sons are accompanied in the afterlife. Yardley is a reporter for The Scotsman, *a Scottish national newspaper published in Edinburgh.*

As you read, consider the following questions:

1. What is the definition Yardley gives for "ancestor worship?"
2. According to Yardley, at what age is a deceased son deemed old enough for a corpse bride?
3. According to the author, why do many men in the Loess Plateau have difficulty meeting women to marry?

For many Chinese, an ancestor is someone to honour, but also someone whose needs must be maintained. Families

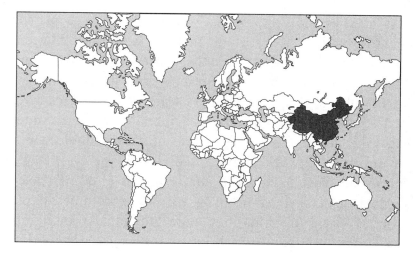

burn offerings, fake money or paper models of luxury cars, in case an ancestor might need pocket change or a stylish ride in the netherworld. But in the parched canyons along the Yellow River known as the Loess Plateau, some parents will go a step further. To ensure a bachelor son's contentment in the afterlife, they will search for a dead woman to be his bride and, once a corpse is obtained, bury the pair together as a married couple.

> *"Traditional Chinese beliefs . . . hold that an unmarried life is incomplete."*

"They happen pretty often, especially when teenagers or younger people die," said Yang Husheng, 48, a travelling funeral director in the region who said he last attended such a ceremony in the spring. "I've been in the business for seven or eight years, and I've seen all sorts of things."

The Custom of Afterlife Marriage Extends from Traditional Beliefs

The rural folk custom is known as minghun, or afterlife marriage. Scholars who have studied it say it is rooted in the Chinese form of ancestor worship, which holds that people continue to exist after death and that the living are obliged to tend to their wants—or risk the consequences. Traditional Chinese beliefs also hold that an unmarried life is incomplete.

In villages across the Loess Plateau, which spreads across parts of Shanxi and Shaanxi Provinces, everyone acknowledges the custom. People say parents of a dead son depend on an informal network of friends or family, or even a well-connected fixer, to locate a family that has recently lost a single daughter. Selling or buying corpses for commercial purposes is illegal in China, but these individual transactions, usually for cash, seem to fall into a fuzzier category and are quietly arranged between families.

In some villages, a son is eligible for such a spouse if he is 12 or older when he dies. No one considers the custom shameful or overly macabre. Instead, it is described as a parental duty reflecting Confucian values about loyalty to family.

"Parents have a sense of responsibility for their son," said one woman, Li Yinlan. She said she had attended ceremonies where the coffins were placed side by side and musicians played a dirge. "They have this custom everywhere," she said of her region.

"A family searching for a female corpse typically must pay more than 10,000 yuan ... almost four years of income for an average farmer."

The Communist Party has tried, with mixed success, to stamp out beliefs it considers to be superstition. But the continued practice of the ancient custom in the Loess Plateau is a testament to the region's extreme isolation. In other parts of rural China, it is difficult to know how often, if at all, the custom is followed.

The Loess Plateau, a dense warren of eroding canyons where some villages are unreachable by road, is separated

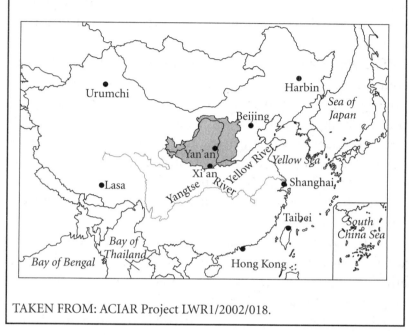

Location of the Loess Plateau along the Yellow River in China Where Obtaining Corpse Brides for Deceased Sons Is Not Uncommon

TAKEN FROM: ACIAR Project LWR1/2002/018.

from much of the change stirring up China. Many young people have fled the arid hills, while those left behind struggle to raise a crop. Many of the men left behind also struggle to find a wife.

A Lack of Women in the Area Provokes the Business of Corpse Brides

The reason is that many women have left for work in cities, never to return, while those women who remain can afford to be picky. No family would approve of a daughter marrying a man too poor to afford a dowry and a decent future. Families of the poorest bachelor sons sometimes pool their savings to buy a wife from bride sellers, the travelling brokers who lure, trick or sometimes kidnap women from other regions and then illegally sell them into marriage.

Villagers from Chenjiayuan, and Yang, the funeral director, said a family searching for a female corpse typically must pay more than 10,000 yuan, or about £650, almost four years of income for an average farmer. Families of the bride regard the money as the dowry they would have received had death not intervened.

The existence of such a market for brides has led to scattered reports of grave robbing. This year, a man in Shaanxi Province captured two men trying to dig up the body of his wife, according to a local news account.

In February, a woman from Yangquan tried to buy the remains of a dead 15-year-old girl, abandoned at a hospital in another city, to satisfy her unmarried deceased brother. She said the brother's ghost was invading her dreams and demanding a wife.

In the village of Qinjiagelao, where roughly one in four eligible men are unmarried, Qin Yuxing, 80, is a genial grandfather unashamed of the minghun practice or the fact that he bought living brides for both his sons.

His younger son, now 40, had tried to find a spouse but the family was too poor.

The elder Qin saved his money and bought a bride from a man who showed up at a local market offering a woman for £270. The woman bore Qin's son a child and then left three years ago to visit her family—and never came back.

Some Kenyan Men Hide the Existence of Multiple Wives

Gakiha Weru and Susan Linee

In the following viewpoint, Gakiha Weru and Susan Linee point out that Kenyan men often marry multiple women, while their first, legitimate wives remain unaware. The authors argue that this secret often remains unbroken until the polygamist husband dies and one or more of his other wives reveal themselves to obtain a share of his inheritance. The authors acknowledge the harsh psychological and legal effects secret polygamy has on wives and children, who suddenly become aware that the men whom they assumed were monogamous actually led double lives. Weru and Linee are journalists for Kenya's The Daily Nation; *published in Nairobi, it is East Africa's most circulated newspaper.*

As you read, consider the following questions:

1. According to Weru and Linee, what does Rev Njoya believe is the cause of secret polygamy?

2. According to the authors, what are some "factors" that provoke secret polygamy among Kenyan husbands?

3. What reasons does marriage counselor Wanjiku Gikang'a give to explain why women become secret brides?

Gakiha Weru and Susan Linee, "Kenya; Secret Wives," *The Daily Nation* (Nairobi), May 4, 2008. Reproduced by permission.

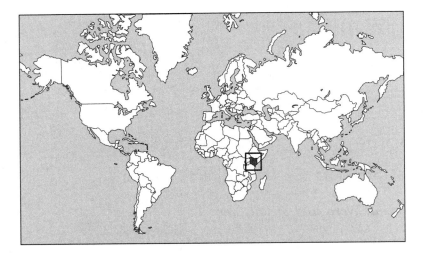

They are wives in secret service. They are faceless and the legally married wives are usually clueless about their existence. Marrying in secret is an art a section of Kenyan men seem to have perfected and the extra wives they marry often become conspirators for a lifetime.

A Common Scenario of How Secret Wives Become Unveiled

The script is almost always the same: a well-to-do man dies. Then cameras zoom in to the sitting room where a distraught widow is giving an account of her husband's last moments in the world and how he was in fact the best husband and father on earth.

The following day's newspapers take cue and quote the fallen man's college-going daughter and teenage son explaining how the pillar of stability in the family has suddenly been snatched by the "cruel hand of death." The body is moved to a funeral home of repute, a necessary ritual to underscore the importance of the fallen man.

A family spokesman, hurriedly appointed to give media updates, will be careful to throw just the right word as he unveils the plan for the man's final journey home—a well-scripted choreography of escorting the departed.

A couple of days later, a bombshell is dropped. The fallen man's wives who served in secret crawl out of the woodwork and hell breaks loose. They give media interviews, run parallel obituaries in the papers, rush to court seeking orders for recognition of their status or a piece of the man's estate and even praying to the court to order the deferment of the man's burial until their status is determined.

In some cases, the other wife or wives is an open secret and all parties tolerate the arrangement. Retired Presbyterian cleric Timothy Njoya, who is now carrying out research on masculinity, says that he has seen it all in decades of ministry where secret families pop up at the funeral.

Inequality in a Patriarchal Society

"I once went to bury a church elder and an older wife appeared with her children," the Rev Njoya told *Sunday Nation* in a telephone interview in May 2008. The retired cleric says that secret polygamy is a result of unbridled appetite by men who feel superior to women, a condition he defines as flawed masculinity.

"'Monogamous instincts conflict with polygamous instincts. Men want to have their cake and eat it.'"

"It is a result of inequality between men and women where a man feels that he needs to eat more and mate more because he is the hunter and gatherer. He is entitled to more and top-ups. But they are mainly hidden because it is ultra vires (not allowed by law)," the Rev Dr Njoya said. "All polygamy is flawed masculinity where men think that women are less human and that one woman cannot be enough," he said. "You will even see a man with two women killing one of them for flirting with another man."

But the cleric warns that hiding a relationship can ruin the family that is left behind by the departing patriarch.

"Monogamous instincts conflict with polygamous instincts. Men want to have their cake and eat it," Rev Njoya said. "If you want to eat more than everyone else but appear as though you took an equal share, you must hide." He says the hiding is a "very violent pathology" because you have two legacies; the apparent monogamous one and the actual polygamous one.

The Psychological Effects of Secret Polygamy

"It will have a psychic effect on the families left behind. A son who thought that his father was monogamous suddenly discovers that it is not true." Rev Njoya has studied the theories of origin of all communities in Kenya and the Ashanti, Gaa and Ewe in Ghana, the Hausa, the Yoruba, the Igbo and the Bakongo in Nigeria and found out that they were predicated on monogamous relationships.

"Distortion, even in Judaism, came later in the medieval times," Rev Njoya said.

Death often triggers unforeseen problems. The other wife will most likely be living in a good neighbourhood. She will have little children going to a good, expensive school, and the death of the "husband" will bring some harsh realities. If her source of income is not commensurate with the kind of lifestyle provided by the "husband," drastic changes in life as known by herself and children are inevitable.

The Question of Inheritance

Then, there is the little matter of property. Since their relationship was of man and wife, to her there is no reason all the property should not end up with just one family—hers. With this, an acrimonious court battle is mapped out. Some of the "other" wives have been known to bide their time till such a time when one of her children, now grown up, springs a nice surprise on the legitimate family years later.

Eighteen years ago, a rich, high ranking government official died. Everything went on all nice and proper, marking the end of a life well lived. That was until a young man showed up to claim his rightful share of his dad's property. Naturally, the matter ended up in court. The young man had a load of documents to prove his claim, including money transfers from his "dad" to pay his fees in an overseas college.

To date, the other family is still fending off a fierce court battle. Last year, the High Court granted the young man's plea to have the remains of his "dad" exhumed to facilitate DNA test to determine paternity. The matter is still in court.

Why Some Kenyan Men Have Secret Wives

Experts say that there are a lot of factors that give rise to this trend, ranging from unhappiness at home, clash between Christianity and centuries-old cultural practices and infidelity. While most communities in Kenya have always practised polygamy, it is outlawed by Christianity and this partly explains why men who decide to take a second wife do it in secret, for fear of being excommunicated, especially if they married the first wife in church.

For those not particularly worried about the church, they simply go the customary way and marry a second wife. But even here the second wife will eventually find herself in trouble in the event of the husband's death.

Advice Against Becoming a Secret Wife

A woman marrying or cohabiting with a married man will eventually find herself in a very precarious position because, in law, she is not recognised and is not entitled to stake a claim on the man's property.

"At the very best, she can be the legal representative of her children," says Ms Jane Onyango, the executive director of the

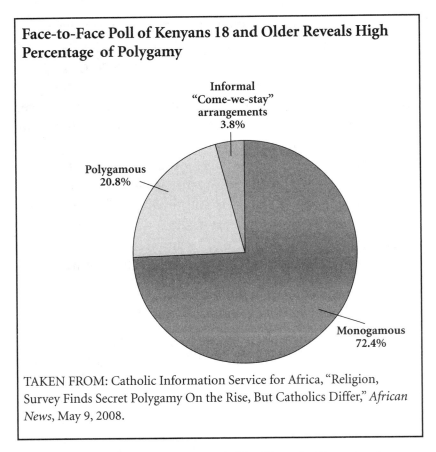

Face-to-Face Poll of Kenyans 18 and Older Reveals High Percentage of Polygamy

Informal
"Come-we-stay"
arrangements
3.8%

Polygamous
20.8%

Monogamous
72.4%

TAKEN FROM: Catholic Information Service for Africa, "Religion, Survey Finds Secret Polygamy On the Rise, But Catholics Differ," *African News*, May 9, 2008.

Federation of Women Lawyers (Fida-Kenya). She says the current trend, where men have secret wives, is a threat to the family. She insists that the legal wife has the responsibility of ensuring the security of her marriage and her family. "It is difficult to keep the existence of another wife absolutely secret. If you hear a turnout, you should investigate and confront your husband with your findings and sort the issues out in order to safeguard your rights."

She advises women against becoming second wives, saying a woman has many choices and being the secret wife should not be one of them.

"If a woman decides to become the second wife, she should ensure that her future and that of her children is secure. She should insist that the man draws a will under which she and the children can get a share of the property," she counsels.

"'It only takes a pot of beer, some goats delivered to the second set of in-laws and a second wife finds her way into the home.'"

Ms Onyango says polygamy, whether recognised or secret, has the potential of causing suffering and should be avoided.

The Importance of Legally Preparing for Marriage

"Women should insist on marriage under the statutory law. The customary marriage has potential of going polygamous and there is little the woman can do. It only takes a pot of beer, some goats delivered to the second set of in-laws, and a second wife finds her way into the home. If you marry under the customary law, you should never close your eyes to this possibility."

Marriage counsellor Wanjiku Gikang'a says the existence of secret wives, who come out the woodwork when the husband dies, is a direct offshoot of failure to understand the institution of marriage and what it entails.

"People get into marriage without any preparation. They expect to receive so much from their partners while they are not ready to give as much in return," she says. When the man finds that he is not getting what he expected, he becomes unhappy with the marriage and might be tempted to look for somebody who fulfils his idea of the ideal wife.

"Many secret wives come into existence this way. If couples went for pre-marital training and counselling they would be better prepared for the hard work that is marriage," the counsellor says. She regrets that society does not disapprove of men keeping secret wives. She says these liaisons are not only immoral but also perpetuate discrimination against women.

"But it's also important to recognise that women willingly get into these situations mostly because the man has money or is prominent and they want a share of the glory. Any time you hear women suddenly showing up with their children in tow, you can be sure the man has a lot money."

While the public might get entertained through the media as wives of a prominent person pop up, Mrs Gikang'a says what is often missed is the pain of the legal wife when confronted by a family whose existence she didn't know.

"First, losing a husband is very painful. It hurts even more because the trust she had for him is shattered. The feeling that he had been cheating on you over the years is traumatising and this makes the healing process slower. This is why the society should fight this trend more vigorously," she says.

Periodical Bibliography

The following articles have been selected to supplement the diverse views presented in this chapter.

Africa News	"Ghana; Child Marriage Still an Issue," August 13, 2007.
Ross Appleyard	"The Child Brides Who Give Themselves to Tradition," *The Times* (London), May 17, 2008.
Nina Bernstein	"Polygamy, Practiced in Secrecy, Follows Africans to New York," *The New York Times*, March 23, 2007.
Kim Hughes	"A Disturbing Trip to Bountiful Abuse in the Name of God; An Angry B.C. Journalist Demands to Know Who is Going to Protect the Young from the Polygamists," *The Toronto Star*, March 30, 2008.
Noor Javed	"I Do, I Do, I Do. The Last Taboo; Multiple Spouses are Fine, Just Not in the West," *Toronto Star*, May 24, 2008.
Nancie L. Katz	"Pakistanis' Secret Shame Parents Force Daughters to Fly Home for Arranged Marriages," *Daily News* (New York), November 25, 2007.
Charles Lewis	"Criminal Act or Religious Right?; Canada Stymied by Polygamy Issue," *National Post* (Canada), August 11, 2007.
New Vision	"Uganda; Is Man Naturally Polygamous?" July 6, 2007.
Shalini Sinha	"Arranged Traditions," *The Irish Times*, December 12, 2006.
UN Integrated Regional Information Networks	"Mali; Child Marriage a Neglected Problem," August 30, 2007.
Jocelyn Voo	"Arranged Marriage Gets High Tech Twist," April 23, 2008. www.cnn.com.

 GLOBALVIEWPOINTS

Same-Sex Marriage

1

Americans Debate
Same-Sex Marriage

Barbara Kantrowitz et al.

*In the following viewpoint, Barbara Kantrowitz and her colleagues report on the diverse American attitudes toward same-sex marriage while arguing that the significant changes to marriage are being made by heterosexuals throughout the world who are moving away from the traditional mold of marriage. According to the authors, much of the Western world accepts and supports same-sex marriage as a basic human right, while many Americans see the traditional face of marriage so changed that they think same-sex marriage would destroy the structure of the institution. *Newsweek *is a weekly newsmagazine based in New York City with eighteen bureaus worldwide.*

As you read, consider the following questions:

1. According to the authors, what is the "Pacte Civil de Solidarite" that France approved in 1998?

2. According to the authors, what percentage of twenty-five- to thirty-four-year-olds are cohabiting in Europe?

3. According to the authors' claims, when did religion begin to influence the institution of marriage?

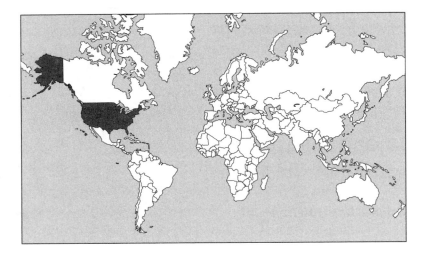

Los Angeles actresses Alice Dodd and Jillian Armenante got married four years ago [2000] at a raucous wedding in New Jersey before 250 friends and family members. Even so, when San Francisco Mayor Gavin Newsom began issuing same-sex marriage licenses in mid-February—in open defiance of California law—the couple drove 650 km north and waited in line for seven hours at city hall to tie the knot again. "Uncle Sam couldn't make it to our first wedding," says Armenante. "We thought it would be nice if he came to our second." They were among the more than 3,000 gay and lesbian couples that had exchanged vows by the end of last week [March 2004], even though it's still not clear whether their marriages will stand up in court.

To supporters of gay rights, the scene was deeply moving: elderly men and women who had spent a lifetime waiting to make their unions legal, parents with infants in their arms, middle-aged lawyers and doctors. But to opponents, the peaceful scene was a provocative call to arms. American conservatives say San Francisco is proof of the anarchy they've predicted if officials act on their own before the legal debate over gay marriage is settled. "There are millions of Americans angry and disgusted by what they see on the TV—two brides, two grooms, but not a man and a woman," says Randy Thomasson, executive director of the Campaign for California Families, which is fighting the San Francisco marriages in court. "This is the new civil war in America."

The issue threatens to be a defining one in the current [2004] U.S. presidential election. Under pressure from his evangelical Christian supporters, President George W. Bush has been dancing around it for months. Although he keeps reiterating his view that marriage should be limited to the union of a man and a woman, he has stopped short of a full public endorsement of a constitutional amendment that would ban same-sex weddings. His most likely Democratic opponent, Massachusetts Sen. John Kerry, has said he opposes gay marriage but thinks the issue is up to each state to decide.

"Much of the rest of the world is watching America's struggle with curiosity. In many places, same-sex marriage is simply a ho-hum issue."

The debate is gaining momentum. Civil unions between same-sex couples are currently legal in only one state—Vermont—but at the end of last week [March 2004] officials in New Mexico's Sandoval County began issuing licenses to gays before being shut down by the state's attorney general. The next move will most likely be in court, not only in California, but also in Massachusetts, where the state's Supreme Judicial Court essentially legalized gay marriage in November. State officials have until mid-May to say how they will comply.

Other Areas of the Western World Legally Recognize Same-Sex Marriage and/or Cohabitation

Much of the rest of the world is watching America's struggle with curiosity. In many places, same-sex marriage is simply a ho-hum issue. Last week even the 81-year-old king of Cambodia, Norodom Sihanouk, said that as a "liberal democracy," his country should allow gays and lesbians to marry. The Netherlands became the first country to legalize same-sex marriages, in 2001; Belgium followed earlier last year [2003], as did two Canadian provinces, Ontario and British Columbia. In Brazil, stable gay and lesbian couples can inherit from each other and claim one another as dependents in tax returns. In the Argentine province Rio Negro and the capital of Buenos Aires, new laws allow registered gay couples to qualify for family welfare payments. While critics contend that same-sex weddings will destroy the "sanctity" of traditional unions, many scholars say that it's actually heterosexual couples who are radically redefining marriage. Many countries, including Norway, Sweden, Denmark and its province Greenland, have registered partnership laws that extend some benefits of marriage to unmarried couples, both gay and straight. Germany has quietly expanded rights for cohabitating couples, while in 1998, France approved the Pacte Civil de Solidarité—a kind of intermediate step between casual cohabitation and formal marriage that provides tax and health benefits. "There is no way to turn back the wheel," says sociologist Dieter Bruhl of Germany's University of Oldenburg. "Today marriage is an institution at the free disposal of individualized members of a highly differentiated society."

The Traditional Family Unit Declines Worldwide

Across the world, the old model—marriage and then kids—has given way to a dizzying array of family arrangements that reflect more lenient attitudes about cohabitation, divorce and illegitimate births. University of Chicago sociologist Linda Waite, author of *The Case for Marriage*, says that gay couples are "really swimming against the tide. What they want is something that maybe heterosexual couples take for granted: the social, religious and legal recognition of a union."

"The institution of marriage is so battered that many consider gay unions the last straw."

On the other hand, this increasingly diverse family album could be one reason why the push for gay marriage has struck a nerve among some social conservatives. The institution of marriage is so battered that many consider gay unions the last straw, says Princeton historian Hendrik Hartog, author of *Man and Wife in America.* "They see gay marriage as a boundary case," he says—in other words, a step too far.

Marriage rates are tumbling virtually everywhere. In 1990, eight out of every 1,000 Brazilians got married; a decade later that number had dropped to 5.7. In Europe as well, marriage rates are plummeting and illegitimate births are increasingly common. Divorce rates are rising; Germany's divorce rate reached a record high last year—and new marriages approached a record low. "We've moved from de jure to de facto marriage," says Kathleen Kiernan of the London School of Economics. She estimates that 50 percent of 25- to 34-year-olds in Europe are cohabiting. The numbers are highest, perhaps 70 percent, in Scandinavia, especially Sweden. The Swedes have even created their own term for someone who cohabits: "sambo" or "living together": a word that appears on official forms besides the options "married" and "single." Another new word, "sarbo," refers to people who consider themselves a couple but live apart.

In many countries, women see little reason to forgo their newly won independence. The number of thirtysomething single women in Japan has increased drastically in recent years. "They don't have a good reason to get married or, rather, a good reason to put a stop to their single lives," says Keiko Oshima, chief planner at Gauss Life Psychology Institute, a marketing agency in Tokyo. A *Yomiuri Shimbun* [a newspaper published in major Japanese cities such as Tokyo] survey conducted in August found that 52 percent of people believed that a woman could be happy without marriage. The same poll found that only 45 percent thought that a man became a "real man" when he had his own family. Nearly one in three Tokyo women in their 30s is unmarried, in a culture where getting married at 25 was once the norm.

Establishing a family used to involve four steps: a marital ceremony, moving in together, beginning a sex life and finally having children. Today couples pick and choose not only the steps but also which will come first. Thirty years ago, says Kiernan, only five of 19 European countries reported 10 percent or more of children born out of wedlock. Today only Greece remains below that threshold, and the European average has jumped to 30 percent.

Those figures are of great concern to researchers, who say that children suffer without the emotional and economic support of two parents—and thrive when reared in stable two-parent families. Married couples tend to have more assets, live longer and are better adjusted emotionally than their single counterparts. Fewer money worries may contribute to that well-being, but having someone around to watch out for you also helps, says Evelyn Lehrer, a professor of economics at the University of Illinois.

The Stability of the Concept of Marriage

While the decline of marriage may seem to portend some kind of social cataclysm, scholars say the institution has always been in flux, responding to the particular needs of different eras. "Throughout much of history, if you acted like you were married, then you were treated like you were married," says marriage historian Stephanie Coontz of Evergreen State University in Washington. Religion, a major part of the current defense of "traditional" marriage, didn't even enter the picture, Coontz says, until the ninth century, and then only to prevent European aristocrats from marrying close relatives.

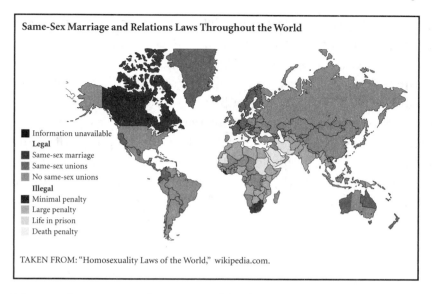

Same-Sex Marriage and Relations Laws Throughout the World

Information unavailable
Legal
Same-sex marriage
Same-sex unions
No same-sex unions
Illegal
Minimal penalty
Large penalty
Life in prison
Death penalty

TAKEN FROM: "Homosexuality Laws of the World," wikipedia.com.

The goal was to make sure noble families didn't consolidate too much power. (Commoners could still hook up with anyone they fancied.)

Even in modern times, traditional marriage has never been a universal institution. Carlos Eroles, a lecturer in social work at the University of Buenos Aires, says that throughout Argentina's history, the lower classes and especially farm laborers tended to cohabit, while the upper classes married. Marriage became more widespread after the influx of millions of immigrants from Spain and Italy, both conservative Roman Catholic countries, during the nineteenth and early twentieth centuries.

What's most amazing, perhaps, is that the ideal of marriage has such staying power. The push by gay activists to gain equal rights in marriage was initially motivated by the desire to obtain the legal benefits of being a spouse, such as health insurance and inheritance rights. But many say that it's equally important to make a public statement of affection and commitment—a view of marriage that crosses political and social boundaries. In 1998, Australian Jackie Stricker married Dr. Kerryn Phelps under a chuppah (the Jewish marriage canopy) in a Park Avenue apartment. "The rabbi read verses from the Book of Ruth: 'Where you go, I will go,'" Stricker recalls. "It was incredibly romantic." The two women are now back in Australia, where gay couples have some limited rights but can't legally marry. "No group in any society should be grateful for crumbs from the table masquerading as grand gestures," says Phelps. "I feel robbed of the language of being married, of being the daughter-in-law, the wife, the aunt, the stepmother." And when the law says "You can't," the sweetest words are "I do."

In the United States, a Same-Sex Marriage Ban Is Overruled

Maura Dolan

In the following viewpoint, Maura Dolan addresses the California Supreme Court's decision to overturn every law that discriminates against a person's sexual preference, including the gay marriage ban. Dolan reports that the decision has made California the second state, behind Massachusetts, to legalize same-sex marriage, rousing both celebration and controversy. According to Dolan, many expect the California ruling to ignite more discussion about legalizing same-sex marriage throughout the United States. Dolan is a writer for the Los Angeles Times, *a daily California newspaper widely distributed throughout the western United States.*

As you read, consider the following questions:

1. According to Dolan, what state besides California allows same-sex marriages?

2. According to the author, though California has overturned the ban on gay marriage, same-sex couples will still not obtain which federal benefits?

3. As recognized by Brad Sears, what court decision "marked gays and lesbians as second-class citizens"?

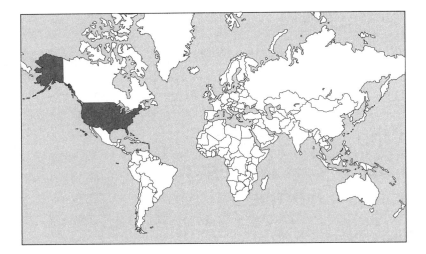

The California Supreme Court struck down the state's ban on same-sex marriage Thursday [May 15, 2008] in a broadly worded decision that would invalidate virtually any law that discriminates on the basis of sexual orientation.

The 4–3 ruling declared that the state Constitution protects a fundamental "right to marry" that extends equally to same-sex couples. It tossed a highly emotional issue into the [2008] election year while opening the way for tens of thousands of gay people to wed in California, starting as early as mid-June.

The majority opinion, by Chief Justice Ronald M. George, declared that any law that discriminates on the basis of sexual orientation will from this point on be constitutionally suspect in California in the same way as laws that discriminate by race or gender, making the state's high court the first in the nation to adopt such a stringent standard.

The decision was a bold surprise from a moderately conservative, Republican-dominated court that legal scholars have long dubbed "cautious," and experts said it was likely to influence other courts around the country.

But the scope of the court's decision could be thrown into question by an initiative already heading toward the November ballot. The initiative would amend the state Constitution to prohibit same-sex unions.

The campaign over that measure began within minutes of the decision. The state's Catholic bishops and other opponents of same-sex marriage denounced the court's ruling. But Gov. Arnold Schwarzenegger, who previously has vetoed two bills in favor of gay marriage, issued a statement saying he "respects" the decision and "will not support an amendment to the constitution that would overturn" it.

Reactions to the 4–3 Ruling

The ruling was greeted with loud cheering and whooping when it was released at the high court's headquarters Thursday morning. About 100 people lined up outside to purchase copies of the decision for $10 apiece. Some people bought 10 to 15 copies, calling it a historic document. One man said he planned to give them out as Christmas presents.

Gay groups planned celebrations up and down the state.

"I can finally say I will be able to marry John, the man that I love," said Stuart Gaffney, one of the plaintiffs in the case, referring to his partner of 21 years, John Lewis. "Today is the happiest and most romantic day of our lives."

"California has more than 100,000 households headed by gay couples, about a quarter with children."

Conservative and religious-affiliated groups denounced the decision and pledged to bring enough voters to the polls in November to overturn it. Mathew Staver, founder of Liberty Counsel, called the decision "outrageous" and "nonsense."

"No matter how you stretch California's Constitution, you cannot find anywhere in its text, its history or tradition that now, after so many years, it magically protects what most societies condemn," Staver said.

The decision came after high courts in New York, Washington and New Jersey refused to extend marriage rights to gay couples. Only Massachusetts' top court has ruled in favor of permitting gays to wed.

The Significance of Wording

The court's ruling repeatedly invoked the words "respect and dignity" and framed the marriage question as one that deeply affected not just couples but also their children. California has more than 100,000 households headed by gay couples, about a quarter with children, according to 2000 census data.

"Our state now recognizes that an individual's capacity to establish a loving and long-term committed relationship with another person and responsibly to care for and raise children does not depend upon the individual's sexual orientation," George wrote for the majority. "An individual's sexual orientation—like a person's race or gender—does not constitute a legitimate basis upon which to deny or withhold legal rights."

Many gay Californians said that even the state's broadly worded domestic partnership law provided only a second-class substitute for marriage. The court agreed.

Giving a different name, such as "domestic partnership," to the "official family relationship" of same-sex couples imposes "appreciable harm" both on the couples and their children, the court said.

The distinction might cast "doubt on whether the official family relationship of same-sex couples enjoys dignity equal to that of opposite-sex couples," George wrote, joined by Justices Joyce L. Kennard, Kathryn Mickle Werdegar and Carlos R. Moreno. All but Moreno were appointed by Republican governors. George was appointed by Gov. Pete Wilson in 1991.

The ruling cited a 60-year-old precedent that struck down a ban on interracial marriage in California.

The Issue Inside the Courtroom

The three dissenting justices argued that it was up to the electorate or the legislature to decide whether gays should be permitted to marry.

In 2000, 61 percent of California voters approved a ballot measure, Proposition 22, that said "only marriage between a man and a woman is valid and recognized in California."

Since then, the legislature has passed one of the strongest domestic partnership laws in the country, giving registered same-sex couples most of the rights of married people.

"In my view, California should allow our gay and lesbian neighbors to call their unions marriage," Justice Carol A. Corrigan wrote in the first sentence of her dissent.

"But I, and this court, must acknowledge that a majority of Californians hold a different view and have explicitly said so by their vote. This court can overrule a vote of the people only if the Constitution compels us to do so. Here, the Constitution does not."

Justice Marvin R. Baxter, joined by Justice Ming W. Chin, said the ruling "creates the opportunity for further judicial extension of this perceived constitutional right into dangerous territory."

"Who can say that in 10, 15 or 20 years, an activist court might not rely on the majority's analysis to conclude, on the basis of a perceived evolution in community values, that the laws prohibiting polygamous and incestuous marriages were no longer constitutionally justified?" Baxter wrote.

Same-Sex Marriages in California Are Not Yet Eligible for All Benefits

The decision takes effect in 30 days. Gay couples would then be permitted to marry in California, even if they do not live in the state, gay rights lawyers said. Under federal law, however, other states would not have to recognize those marriages as valid. And same-sex couples would remain ineligible for certain federal benefits, including Social Security benefits for spouses and joint filing for income taxes.

Lawyers on both sides of the debate said they were uncertain how a victory for the proposed November initiative—which both sides predict will qualify for the ballot—would affect gay couples who marry during the next several months.

University of Santa Clara law professor Gerald Uelmen, who has closely followed the state high court for decades, said he was "blown away" and "very surprised" by the ruling.

"The court is exerting some leadership here, and I think it needs to be said that it is a new role for the court," Uelmen said.

"This has not been a court that has been willing to stick its neck out and lead the way on cutting-edge issues like this that involve such strong political feelings."

Court's Decision as a Reflection of the Choice of Many Californians

Uelmen said the court's vote probably reflected the fact that a growing number of Californians favor marriage for gay couples. He noted the case attracted a record number of friend-of-the-court briefs, most of them in favor of same-sex marriage.

"[Law professor Kermit] Roosevelt predicted more states would follow California's example and that the U.S. Supreme Court would eventually rule in favor of same-sex marriage."

Although critics of the ruling, including the dissenters, argued the court should have waited for the voters to decide the question of same-sex marriage, "the majority is not always supposed to have its way" in constitutional democracies, said

University of Pennsylvania constitutional law professor Kermit Roosevelt, one of many legal scholars who weighed in on the case Thursday.

Roosevelt predicted more states would follow California's example and that the U.S. Supreme Court would eventually rule in favor of same-sex marriage.

"That decision will come at the end of a process that is now just beginning," Roosevelt said. He predicted it would follow the pattern of state courts that struck down laws banning interracial marriage decades ago.

The decision followed several recent rulings by the state high court recognizing the rights of same-sex parents, including those not biologically related to their children. The children in those families figured prominently in the court's reasoning in those cases.

Historical Background of Ruling 4–3

The road to Thursday's [May 2008] ruling began with San Francisco's highly publicized same-sex weddings, which in 2004 helped spur a conservative backlash in an election year and a national dialogue over gay rights.

Several states later passed constitutional amendments banning gay marriage, and same-sex marriage became an issue in the race for president.

After a month of jubilant gay weddings here, the California Supreme Court intervened and ordered the city to stop issuing licenses to same-sex couples.

The state high court later invalidated the licenses, saying the city should have waited for a judicial ruling before acting.

The plan by San Francisco Mayor Gavin Newsom, City Atty. Dennis Herrera and gay rights lawyers to challenge state law by marrying same-sex couples was carefully drawn.

City officials chose the first couples to wed, hoping their long unions and sympathetic stories would put a face on same-sex marriage that courts would find difficult to reject.

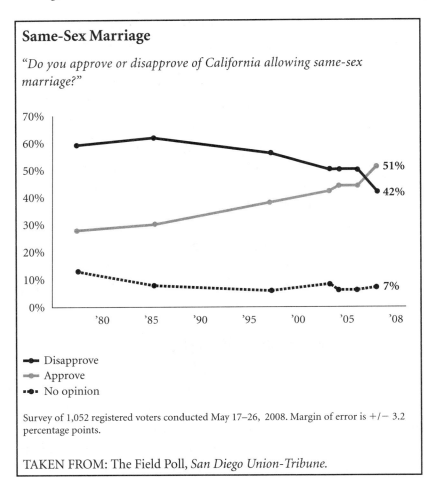

Same-Sex Marriage

"Do you approve or disapprove of California allowing same-sex marriage?"

- ● Disapprove
- ● Approve
- ● No opinion

Survey of 1,052 registered voters conducted May 17–26, 2008. Margin of error is +/− 3.2 percentage points.

TAKEN FROM: The Field Poll, *San Diego Union-Tribune.*

The city also decided to begin the weddings on a day when courts were closed to deprive opponents of quick legal intervention. One of the first couples to wed has since separated.

The long parade of weddings at City Hall—across the street from the California Supreme Court—provided a dramatic backdrop for the gay rights debate.

As the issue moved into the high court, Brad Sears, executive director of the Williams Institute at UCLA's [University of California, Los Angeles] law school, which examines sexual orientation and the law, said the state's broad domestic partner law had undercut the traditional argument that children were better off being raised by opposite-sex parents.

"Taking those issues off the table, which the domestic partners act did, might have made this an easier case for everyone," Sears said. Once the state recognized the right of gays to rear children, the fight for same-sex marriage was shaped as "the right to have a family" and the ruling became "about family being protected."

The court concluded that giving gays a separate institution—domestic partnership—"marked gays and lesbians as second-class citizens," Sears said.

The Massachusetts high court ruling that permitted gays there to marry did not give sexual orientation the same kind of constitutional protection that Thursday's decision did, nor was the Massachusetts ruling as explicit in stating that marriage licenses must be given to same-sex couples in the immediate future, legal analysts said.

The Issue of Same-Sex Marriage in America Gains Momentum

Sears said recent polls show that Californians are divided over same-sex marriage. Forty-three percent of Californians supported gay marriage in a Field poll taken a year ago.

He added that the issue was likely to affect the political debate even outside California.

"It is going to give some new teeth to an issue that was losing its potency in terms of being a wedge issue," Sears said.

Canadian Gay Men and Women Offer Different Perspectives on Same-Sex Marriage

Sara Wilson

In the following viewpoint, Sara Wilson argues that many perspectives on legalized same-sex marriages exist in the gay and lesbian community of Toronto, Canada. According to Wilson, more same-sex marriages have occurred in Toronto—where gay marriage has been legal since 2003—than anywhere else in North America. Wilson asks six same-sex couples what the legalization of same-sex marriage means to them, dividing the couples into categories: "the radicals," "the enthusiasts," "the idealists," "the feminists," "the long-time companions," and "the newlyweds." Wilson writes for Toronto Life, *Toronto's city magazine.*

As you read, consider the following questions:

1. According to Wilson, Brandon Sawh does not like calling marriage an "institution" but rather believes it is about what?

2. According to the article, what does "being a married woman" sound like to Karen Andrews?

3. According to the article, what does marriage mean to Jim O'Neill?

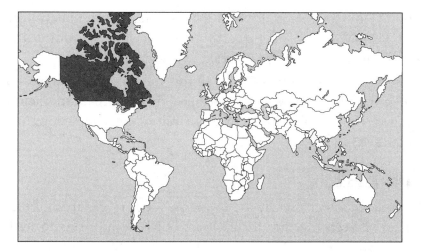

Toronto is the gay marriage capital of North America. More same-sex couples have tied the knot here than anywhere else on the continent: at press time [2005], 2,233 since June 10, 2003, when Ontario expanded the province's definition of marriage to include gay and lesbian unions.

Adam and Steve can now officially wed in seven provinces and one territory. And a final parliamentary vote could make Canada the third country in the world—along with Belgium and the Netherlands to enshrine gay marriage in statute law.

So how has all this same-sex vow making changed the city? In two years, a small army of gay-branded wedding planners, suppliers, Web sites, shows and merchandise sporting a Carson Kressley sensibility has emerged, seducing the altar-bound into ever more elaborate ceremonies. The legislation has also given our battle-scarred tourist industry a serious boost (almost half the gay couples who have gotten hitched in Hogtown so far have been foreigners).

But more significantly, same-sex marriage has changed the fabric of gay relationships. Questions that used to be the exclusive province of boy-girl nuptials are suddenly cropping up on Church Street: Is he the one? When will she pop the question? How long should we date before making the pilgrimage to Tiffany's? And new questions are arising, including the sticky matter of who proposes.

We asked six couples what all this means to their lives, and how the option to wed has changed their intimate moments, expectations and goals. Here, a portrait of gay coupledom in a new age.

The Radicals

Frank and Joel met at a gay men's support group in 1982. They've been together for 23 years but have no plans to wed. They share a four-bedroom Victorian in Cabbagetown. They both wear rings, though there was no ceremony involved in the exchange.

Frank Chester, 49, executive director of a gay rights organization

When I met Joel, he was a practising Orthodox Jew looking for an established doctor or lawyer, and I was the opposite—a WASP and a party person. We pursued the kinds of people we thought we'd be interested in, but we were actually falling in love. I was married for over a year to a woman before I came to terms with my sexuality. We wanted to make it work but couldn't, so my experience of marriage wasn't positive. Also, my parents were divorced when I was in Grade 5, and I had to stand in front of a judge and say who I wanted to live with. I've met married couples who have wonderful relationships; I just don't think any magic happens when you get married.

Joel Rotstein, 52, graphic designer

Frank and I have been together for over two decades. What would be the benefit of getting married? We have a wonderful, loving relationship. We're good friends, we share a home, and our friends recognize us as a couple without us having to have a marriage. We also have an open relationship.

I get something from casual sex partners that Frank can never give me: new relationship energy. Straight people do this as well; they're just not open about it. Having to divorce your wife just because you want to see another woman naked—how stupid is that? Marriage is a sad institution really.

The Enthusiasts

Michael and Keith met in 1996 at Fashion Cares, a fundraiser for AIDS research; Keith was a model in the show. They were married on May 16, 2004, by a Unitarian minister, at a 90-person wedding in the Brassaii restaurant courtyard. They share a three-bedroom house in Little Italy.

"A lot of gays and lesbians see marriage as a sellout, but for me it came down to following my heart."

Michael Battista, 40, immigration lawyer

After the court decision, I started reading about the issue secretly, so Keith wouldn't know what I was considering. A lot of gays and lesbians see marriage as a sellout, but for me it came down to following my heart: I wanted to do something that would make Keith know how much I love him. Walking along King Street right before the wedding, we turned a corner and saw family and friends burst into applause, and I had a sense of who we were as a couple: not just Keith and Michael, but Keith and Michael together. That night, as I was dancing with my six-year-old niece, I thought, I never, ever imagined I'd be dancing with my niece at my wedding.

Keith Maidment, 40, firefighter

We were walking along the coast in India the night Michael proposed. The sea was crashing and all the stars were out, and suddenly Michael was on one knee. We had exchanged Paloma Picasso white gold rings earlier in our relationship, and Michael had sent them to the jeweller to be matted—or so I

115

thought. Turns out he'd had diamonds embedded into them. I started bawling so hard it took me several minutes to say yes. Afterward, we toasted each other with champagne, then phoned our families and friends. They were overjoyed. At the wedding, I drank spritzers all night because I wanted to be able to remember everything.

The Idealists

Brandon and Ryan met at Fly, a Gloucester Street gay bar, in 2003 and started dating soon after. They share a two-bedroom condo at King and John with one roommate and their dog, a Jack Russell-chihuahua cross named Jaz. They exchanged rings engraved with R [love] B and B [love] R on their six-month anniversary. They plan to wed but haven't yet set a date.

Ryan Sanders, 25, IT coordinator

I grew up in Slave Lake, Alberta, and met Brandon three months after moving to Toronto. We weren't looking for relationships, just sex. But after we started hanging out, we wanted more. When you find someone, you just know. My parents were happy about me moving in with Brandon. My mom always wanted somebody to take care of me. Brandon and I have looked at wedding rings at Tiffany's and Birks and Holt's. Salespeople have been helpful everywhere except for just one woman in a mall who walked away. If we were married, family members would recognize us more, I think. And employers might, and politicians. Plus, we want to adopt. We want a couple of kids.

Brandon Sawh, 23, event coordinator

I've always known I was gay, but I was raised Catholic and imagined settling down with the kids, the house and the cottage. And now I can do that with someone I love. Calling marriage "this institution" makes it sound like a prison. Marriage is about respect for the partner. My sister is married, and my brother will one day be married. I don't see why I should be different. After I met Ryan, my mom said, "Wait a year to get married," but now she calls all the time to ask, "When's the wedding?" We'll wait until the law passes in Canada. Then I'll plan the wedding. I see it on a beach: sunset, white lilies, khaki pants, white shirts. Simple rings. More spiritual than formal. Then just a really good feast.

The Feminists

Shelley and Karen first met in 1988, when Karen came to speak at Osgoode Hall about health benefits for same-sex couples. Their paths crossed again when Shelley was Karen's law professor in the early '90s. Shelley had a daughter, Amy, with a partner who died in 1993. She started seeing Karen in 1994, and they moved in together two years later. Shelley's family adores Karen, but Karen hasn't spoken to her family since 1977. They share a large semi at College and Dovercourt with Amy, now 18, and a cat named Toby. They have decided never to marry.

"Marriage is a restrictive, anachronistic patriarchal institution, deeply implicated in the oppression of women and children. Everything should be done to minimize its importance."

Shelley Gavigan, 53, law professor

I grew up Catholic in Saskatchewan and came of age in the late '60s, early '70s, and was part of a wave of women who tried to live differently and think about relationships differently. I take strong exception to the idea that marriage means commitment and that if you're not married you're not committed. It's true that marriage has changed. We now speak of spouses and partners instead of husbands and wives, but marriage is still very gendered and substantively unequal. If I'm invited to a wedding, I'll go and behave myself and wish the couple well, but I don't like the ritual around it—the garter and the crawling under the wedding dress. With our daughter, Amy, if she decides to get married, that's her call. But we'll have to tranquillize Karen.

Karen Andrews, 45, legal clinic lawyer

It means a lot to me that I am an unmarried woman. Being a married woman sounds to me like you're an appendage, that you have lost independence and become your mother. I was always keenly aware that my mother referred to herself as Mrs. Ernest W. Andrews, which I thought was bizarre. I have devoted my career to pushing for gay rights—for social benefits, income tax deductions, health benefits, hospital and prison visitation. Not the right to marry. Marriage is a restrictive, anachronistic patriarchal institution, deeply implicated in the oppression of women and children. Everything should be done to minimize its importance. As a lesbian, you get to live differently, and that should be celebrated. Shelley and I are both magnificent spinsters.

The Long-Time Companions

Patrick and Jim met at The Quest, a gay bar that used to be at Yonge and Charles, in 1973. They've been together ever since and share a two-storey Tudor-style house in Etobicoke, near the lake. They have a Belgian Malinois named Spencer. They have no plans to wed.

Patrick Conlon, 61, author and journalist

We're advocates of the legislation, but personally we're ambivalent. I decided to spend my life with Jim a long time ago. A civil ceremony would simply acknowledge what's already been in place. Two and a half years ago, Jim was hit with acute respiratory distress syndrome and spent 15 weeks in hospital. I was involved in every aspect of his care, and at no time was I made to feel like someone who wasn't significant to him in the married sense of the word. There have been mornings I've looked across the newspaper at Jim and

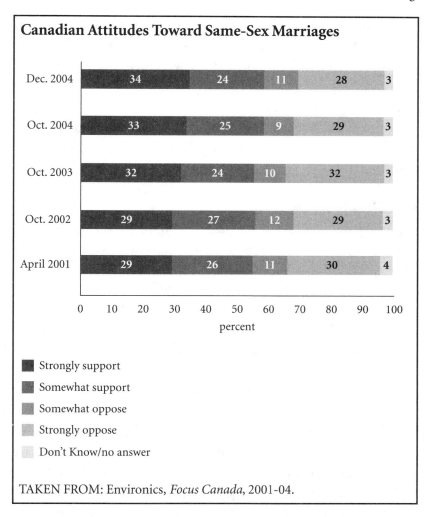

Canadian Attitudes Toward Same-Sex Marriages

	Strongly support	Somewhat support	Somewhat oppose	Strongly oppose	Don't Know/no answer
Dec. 2004	34	24	11	28	3
Oct. 2004	33	25	9	29	3
Oct. 2003	32	24	10	32	3
Oct. 2002	29	27	12	29	3
April 2001	29	26	11	30	4

percent

■ Strongly support
■ Somewhat support
■ Somewhat oppose
□ Strongly oppose
□ Don't Know/no answer

TAKEN FROM: Environics, *Focus Canada*, 2001-04.

said, "F--- 'em, let's go get married." But anger isn't the right reason to do it. After 32 years, we've worked out a whole bunch of stuff that some married couples don't even begin to know about.

Jim O'Neill, 59, antiques consultant

I was 23 years old in 1968, when Trudeau decriminalized homosexuality. Patrick and I both grew up in the Catholic Church and are enormously angry at it. The more you listen to hateful diatribes, the more angry you become. When my siblings were married, it was just automatically celebrated. If Patrick and I chose to get married, that would never be the case. One of my nieces asked if we were going to get married and said, "It's a good way to get some new towels!" But apart from that, I can't think of a motive for being married. To us, marriage doesn't mean anything we don't already have. We are married, as far as we're concerned. Still, we could use some new towels.

The Newlyweds

Janis and Diane met at a fundraiser at El Convento Rico on College Street in 1995. They started dating a couple months later. In 2002, they had a son, Eli Purdy-Flacks, who was conceived by artificial insemination (the father is a friend) and carried by Diane. They exchanged rings on their fourth anniversary, the same rings they used when they got married August 6, 2004, in a 12-person City Hall ceremony, followed by a reception for 35 at Matignon restaurant. They share a three-bedroom row house in Cabbagetown.

Janis Purdy, 38, associate director of a not-for-profit organization

We'd just had Eli when marriage was legalized, and we considered it. We wanted legal status for his sake. But we were so busy and tired we barely had time to think. We used to laugh that our to-do list was buy bread, get a new roof and get married. The election was the tipping point. Polls were indicating that Stephen Harper [leader of the Conservative Party of Canada, he is the 22nd Prime Minister of Canada] was winning, and we felt we'd be foolish if we'd had the opportunity to get married and hadn't taken it. So we booked the wedding. I'm realistic about what marriage is. It's important to a lot of people, but it's not what everyone wants. Still, when I heard the words "We are gathered together here . . ." at our ceremony, I burst into tears. I had grown up thinking they could never be spoken about me.

Diane Flacks, 39, writer and actor

At my sister's wedding, Janis wasn't at the head table with me. We were told it wasn't because we were lesbians but because we weren't married. That was wrong, but there is something powerful about marriage. When you're not married and you have to check a box, you check "single" even if you've been with someone for 15 years. After we had Eli, we listed the pros and cons of getting married. For a while, it seemed as if all our friends who married broke up within a year. We used to joke that it was the kiss of death. But we got caught up in wedding fever and thought, Oh, the romance of it! Then Janis gave me a card with a picture of herself and me and Eli on it that said "Will you marry me?"

South Africans Debate Whether Same-Sex Marriage Is African

Kgomotso Nyanto

In the following viewpoint, Kgomotso Nyanto contends that South Africa's legalization of gay marriage has led many Africans to protest on religious and cultural grounds and to ask whether same-sex marriage is characteristically "African." According to Nyanto, many South Africans are proud that their government is accepting of an individual's sexual preference, while others claim that same-sex marriage cannot be African because of the gender roles that play important parts in the tradition of marriage. Still others are influenced by the marriage market and hope to cash in on new clients. Nyanto is a reporter for New African, *a monthly news magazine headquartered in London, England.*

As you read, consider the following questions:

1. According to Nyanto, why does Tsietsi Tolo think the Bible should not be used as a reason for why same-sex marriage should be illegal?

2. According to the article, what opinion does Nokuzola Mndende have about accepting "black African same-sex couples"?

Kgomotso Nyanto, "South Africa: It Might Be the Law, But Are Gay Marriages Really African?" *New African*, vol. 22, January 2007, p. 22. Copyright © 2007 IC Publications Ltd. Reproduced by permission.

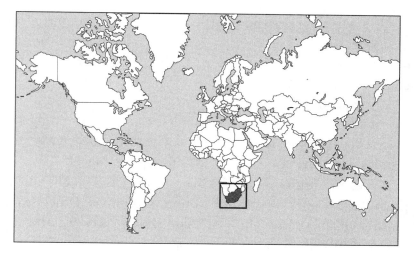

3. According to Nyanto, what characterizes the South African constitution, making it important for communities to "engage themselves in a way that accommodates external pressures"?

It all began with the constitution adopted by a post apartheid dispensation keen to stamp out discrimination in whatever form. Among others, the constitution prohibited discrimination based on sexual orientation.

"The court found that the common law definition of marriage in the Marriage Act of 1961 was inconsistent with the constitution, and invalid to the extent that it did not permit same-sex couples to enjoy the status, benefits and responsibilities it accords to heterosexual couples."

Last year [2006], gay activists decided to put it to the test, and argued in the country's highest court—the Constitutional Court—that it was discriminatory to deny them the right to marry. This was in the historic case of the *Gay Equality Project and Eighteen Others v the Minister of Home Affairs and Others.*

The court agreed and instructed parliament to amend the Marriage Act by 1 December 2006 to recognise civil unions between people of the same sex. The court found that the common law definition of marriage in the Marriage Act of 1961 was inconsistent with the constitution, and invalid to the extent that it did not permit same-sex couples to enjoy the status, benefits and responsibilities it accords to heterosexual couples. Now the cat has been set among the pigeons.

Chief protestors were religious groups. Next in the queue [line] were traditionalists and cultural groupings. Others were those in plain shock. The Christian Action Network and the Islamic Unity Convention have proposed a referendum as well as a constitutional amendment to have marriage only between heterosexual couples. The Islamic Unity Convention lamented: "In Islamic terms, the amendment means putting a halaal [permissible in terms of Islamic Law] stamp on pork."

However, the Commission on Gender Equality has argued that the bill is based on the negative stereotyping of same-sex relationships and that excluding gay relationships from the provisions of the Marriage Act was offensive.

Opinions Clash on Same-Sex Marriage in South Africa

The ANC [African National Congress] MP [Member of Parliament], Tsietsi Tolo, warned against using the Bible to justify the opposition to same-sex marriages, as "the Bible was used to justify apartheid" [social and political policy of racial segregation from 1948–1994 in South Africa]. Tolo also asked the Christian groups whether they wanted parliament to simply ignore the Constitutional Court, which had ruled that same-sex couples should be allowed to enjoy the privileges of marriage and gave parliament a year to change the legislation in line with this ruling.

Public opinion on the subject has sometimes been rabid. In a survey conducted by a local newspaper, a respondent said: "Soon humans will be able to marry cats, dogs and ponies . . . and then evolve into a super species and marry whales, dolphins and sharks—we are one after all."

In rebuttal, another respondent fired some hot salvos: "Let people do what they want, man. I have seen nothing from 'supposedly normal' marriages to suggest that it's anything but a crap institution. I reckon same-sex marriages cannot, possibly, do worse. So let people be."

Some people have chosen to see the money. Businesses, eyeing the till, have been quick off the mark. Wedding planners have established companies specialising in gay marriages. Hotels have also revised their business plans to accommodate the spending power of an emboldened gay movement. Soon one will not be surprised to see two men or women kissing in the lobby or the bar. Churches reported high levels of interest in gay weddings and some, like the Glorious Light Church in Pretoria [located in the northern part of Gauteng Province, it is one of three capital cities], have already officiated over some same-sex marriages. The Home Affairs Department has also been busy, conducting marriages at offices countrywide.

"[According to African custom,] there are gender-linked roles, responsibilities and ceremonies for couples to perform."

However, many churches have flatly refused to associate themselves with what they consider a modern-day Sodom and Gomorrah [sinfulness and sexual deviation].

For Some South Africans, It Is a Question of Tradition

Then there is the controversy in relation to African custom, where there are gender-linked roles, responsibilities and ceremonies for couples to perform.

The traditionalist, Nokuzola Mndende, director of the Icamagu Institute, has said that "legalising same-sex marriages is an insult to our culture as black people." She added that it would be difficult to accept black same-sex couples because there were gender roles, both social and spiritual, for a married couple.

She continued: "If an umakoti (bride) is now a man, how are we going to perform the rituals and the ceremonies? First, when a man announces that he wants to marry, there is a process of ukucela intombi (asking for the bride) and the families meet. Who is now going to be unozakuzaku (delegation that negotiates the bride price, lobolo), for a man who wants to marry another man? Normally it is the man who pays lobolo, but in this case, who is going to pay it?"

Mndende expressed her disappointment with black judges who seemed to kowtow to an "imported, immoral constitution." She said she was frustrated that the government, although black-led, was trying so hard to destabilise tradition.

"Whose Constitution Is It Anyway?"

Dr Mongezi Guma, of the Commission for the Promotion and Protection of the Rights of Cultural, Religion and Linguistic Communities, on the other hand, said cultural practices were inventions by communities, so communities can make adjustments as they respond to pressures.

"To say 'no, it's not cultural' is natural and expected, but communities will need to engage themselves in a way that accommodates external pressures because our constitution forces us to revisit and examine how we relate to one another," said Guma. "Culture was not as static as many people wanted to believe. Communities have had ways of accommodating emerging challenges within a culture. For instance, cattle were used before as a way of paying lobolo, but today money and cheques with receipts are used. So this is one way that communities have accommodated culture," Guma added.

Marginalising Gay People in Botswana May Lead to an Increase in HIV/AIDS

[Christine Stegling, the director of Botswana Network of Ethics, Law and AIDS (BONELA) said] ". . . It is also important to note that the current discrimination and marginalisation faced by the non-heterosexual community needs to be addressed in general, not just the issue of marriage." She warned that if gay people continue to feel marginalised or discriminated, they will not feel comfortable to seek HIV treatment in public health services or the tools that might prevent HIV.

Mmegi,
"Botswana; Botswana Gays Rejoice as Opponents See Red,"
Africa News, *November 17, 2006.*

The rest of Africa also had its say in the survey. Taxi driver, Nicklaus Mwanaseri, in the Tanzanian capital of Dar es Salam, said the decision to allow gays to wed was so immoral that it signified the world was coming to an end. "I see a big flood coming soon because of going against God's teaching," he said.

But gay rights groups dismissed charges that gay marriages were un-African and hoped the decision would pave the way for fairer treatment for homosexuals in Africa.

"I feel very, very proud for South Africans. It is a great model for us, for Africa," said Laurent Laroche, spokesperson for the Mauritian gay rights group, Collectif Arc-en-Ciel.

South Africa's constitution, the supreme law of the land, seeks to resolve such controversies.

But whose constitution is it anyway? The history of South Africa has ensured a multicultural society that seeks to balance every right under the sun. The result, as in this gay saga, demonstrates the enormous difficulties in finding common ground in a cobbled South Africa—a fractured society defined along the lines of race, religion, identities, sub-cultures, sexual orientation, class and every conceivable categorisation.

At the end of the day, if the constitution belongs to no one rather than the fictional everyone, it might just go a long way to resolve many more controversies yet to come.

Senegal Citizens Object to Same-Sex Marriage

Hamadou Tidiane Sy

In the following viewpoint, Hamadou Tidiane Sy argues that published photographs of what is speculated to have been a gay marriage celebration have raised debate about same-sex marriage. Sy reports on the arrests of at least seven people supposedly celebrating a gay marriage in Dakar, West Africa, after a photograph in a local magazine revealed the celebration. According to Sy, the publication director of the magazine has received death threats for publishing the photos from people who deny homosexuality exists locally. Sy notes that in the mostly Muslim Senegal, homosexuality has long carried a social stigma, adding to controversy over publication of the photograph. Sy is a journalist based in Dakar, Senegal, and writes for The Nation, *an African newspaper published in Nairobi.*

As you read, consider the following questions:

1. In the opinion of the author, what debate does same-sex marriage provoke in Africa?

2. According to Sy, what percentage of Senegal's population is Muslim?

3. According to the author, how do the "Goorjigeen," or "biologically effeminate people," fit into Senegalese tradition?

Hamadou Tidiane Sy, "Scandal over Gay Marriage Rocks Country," *The Nation*, February 6, 2008. Reproduced by permission.

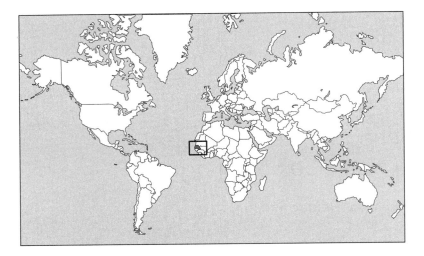

Police in Senegal have arrested at least seven people allegedly involved in the celebration of a gay marriage in a restaurant in the outskirts of Dakar [a port on the Atlantic
Ocean, Dakar is the capital of Senegal, West Africa], raising
again debate about morality and individual freedom in a country caught between conservatism and the desire to project a
tolerant image.

The identities of the people, who are under police custody
but not charged yet, were not revealed, except for one, Pape
Mbaye, who is unknown to the public but whose name has
been given by one newspaper with no further details about his
profile.

The arrest took place on Sunday, following the publication
by a glossy magazine of pictures allegedly taken during the
celebration of the alleged same-sex marriage.

The local press and other Web sites indicate that at least
five of the people arrested appear in the pictures published in
the latest issue of glossy monthly magazine, *Icone*, specialising
in Dakar's trends, nightlife, and jet-setters.

Mr Mansour Dieng, the publication director of *Icone* told
the local media: "When we published the story (of the gay
marriage) in a previous issue, we were treated as liars and ac-

cused of fabricating the story, we have decided to publish the photos to give the public an evidence of what we reported".

Death Threats

Mr Dieng claimed to have received death threats following the publication of the pictures which show a group of dressed up and happy males.

Mr Dieng has since reported to police about the death threats.

In the pictures, one of the suspects appears to be putting a ring on his partner's finger. The alleged gay marriage was between a young Senegalese national and another West African citizen, believed to have gone into hiding since the affair was made public.

With the police not making any official and public statement on the matter, the exact nationality of the runaway suspect is the subject of contradicting reports, some saying he is a Ghanaian national while others identify him as an Ivorian.

Due to the same silent attitude from the police, it was also difficult to clearly establish if the arrests were linked to the celebration of the marriage, to the death threats or to both.

According to *l'Observateur*, a private daily, same-sex marriages are not allowed by Senegalese law.

The newspaper quoted a lawyer as saying "any offender faces up to five years in prison and FCFA 1.5 million fine (US $3,600)" fine.

In Senegal, a nation where Muslims represent more than 95 percent of the population, homosexuality has always been a marginal, sensitive and highly taboo affair.

Though, the phenomenon is known and has always existed, it is totally rejected as contrary to morality and religion.

One pro-islamic NGO [non-governmental organization], Jamra, has issued a statement denouncing the threats against Mr Dieng, the publication director.

Reactions from Dakar, Senegal, Two Weeks After Controversial Photos Were Released

In the weeks since a monthly magazine published photos of what it said was a marriage ceremony between two men in Senegal, the issue of homosexuality has been all over the news in the largely Islamic country. . . .

On call-in shows, many Senegalese are expressing shock over the reported gay marriage and the presence of homosexuals in the country.

Naomi Schwartz,
"Gay Wedding Stirs Controversy in Senegal,"
The Nation, *February 6, 2008.*

But, the NGO also warned the country against the development of "sexual depravation, caused by the greed for easy money and which threatens the country's youth".

The "Goorjigeen" (the name for biologically effeminate people) did exist in Senegalese traditional societies where they were somehow tolerated but not respected nor given any right to exhibit their sexual preferences. They were rather considered as really marginal human beings.

"In local Web sites and newspapers many people are expressing outrage and shock, saying these 'foreign' practices should not be allowed to prosper in the country, while others denounce the hypocrisy of a society which has no courage to face itself."

According to popular belief many of the homosexuals who voluntarily engage in same-sex practices in the big cities adhere to this way of life simply to make money, and the practice itself is at times easily confused with prostitution.

In local Web sites and newspapers many people are expressing outrage and shock, saying these "foreign" practices should not be allowed to prosper in the country, while others denounce the hypocrisy of a society which has no courage to face itself.

Last year a group of young female dancers, including Ndèye Guèye considered as one of the top dancers in the country, was arrested and tried for featuring in a video showing suggestive dance moves.

The video was dubbed indecent and compared to pornography by some people.

At the trial, all dancers were released and put "under probation" but the organisers of the private party and the owner of the club where it took place and where the video was shot were sentenced to prison terms.

Aruba Refuses to Recognize Same-Sex Marriages

The Daily Journal

In the following viewpoint, the author argues that although the Netherlands required Aruba to recognize same-sex marriages, the island territory asserts that their semiautonomous government does not have to recognize local or Dutch same-sex marriages. The author reports on the situation of a lesbian couple legally wed in the Netherlands attempting to register as married in Aruba, a Dutch territory. Their registration was rejected. The Daily Journal *is an English-language daily Latin American newspaper published since 1945.*

As you read, consider the following questions:

1. According to *The Daily Journal*, although Holland legalized gay marriage in 2001 and requires Aruba to acknowledge their legal documents, what is Aruba's argument?

2. According to the publication, what percentage of Aruba's ninety-seven thousand people are Catholic?

3. According to the publication, what normal rights of heterosexual married couples have been denied to Charlene and Ester Oduber-Lamers' same-sex marriage?

The Daily Journal, "Gay Marriage Causes Rift Between Conservatives," August 21, 2005. Reproduced by permission.

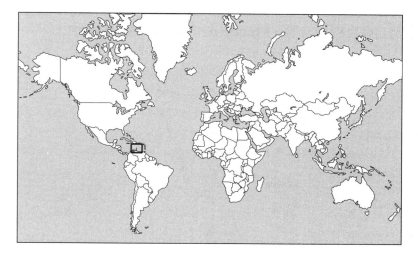

When two women tried to register as a married couple in Aruba, people on this Dutch Caribbean island threw stones at them, slashed their car tires and protested against gay unions outside Parliament.

The hostility eventually led Charlene and Esther Oduber-Lamers to flee the Dutch territory, which refused to recognize their marriage even though the couple legally wed in Holland four years ago.

"I couldn't sleep anymore," Charlene, a 33-year-old Aruba native, said in a phone interview from Holland, where the couple has been living since November. "I felt like maybe they wanted to kill us."

Now the women are locked in a legal battle with Aruba's government to win acceptance of their union in a case that could reach the Supreme Court and force Aruba to recognize gay marriages from Holland.

Dutch and Caribbean Cultures Collided

Their struggle has ignited strong emotions among locals who oppose same-sex marriage, highlighting a deep cultural rift liberal Holland and its former Caribbean colony.

135

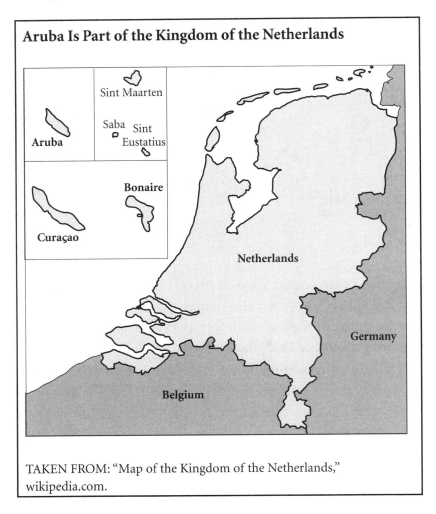

Aruba Is Part of the Kingdom of the Netherlands

TAKEN FROM: "Map of the Kingdom of the Netherlands," wikipedia.com.

Gay marriage was a leading topic of debate on Aruba until recently, when the issue was eclipsed by the search for Natalee Holloway, a U.S. teenager who vanished on May 30 [2005] after leaving a bar with three local men on the final night of a high school graduation trip to the island.

After the Public Registry rejected their marriage certificate, the couple sued Aruba's government for discrimination and a court on the island ruled that their union should be recognized. A judge is to rule on a government appeal of that decision on Aug. 23 [2005] but authorities have vowed to take the matter to the Supreme Court in the Netherlands if necessary, arguing the issue strikes at the very heart of Aruban life. "If we accept gay marriage, would we next have to accept Holland's marijuana bars and euthanasia?" said Ruben Trapenberg, spokesman for Aruban Prime Minister Nelson Oduber. "They have their culture, we have ours."

"Holland legalized gay marriage in 2001, but Aruba's government argues that Dutch law also grants the island the right to self-rule—permitting it not to recognize same-sex unions."

Aruba, a former Dutch colony off the northern coast of Venezuela, is an autonomous republic that forms part of the kingdom of the Netherlands. Dutch statutes require that all members of the Kingdom, Aruba, Holland and the Dutch Antilles, recognize each other's legal documents, including marriage certificates.

Holland legalized gay marriage in 2001, but Aruba' government argues that Dutch law also grants the island the right to self-rule—permitting it not to recognize same-sex unions.

"We can't let this become a precedent," said Hendrik Croes, a lawyer for Aruba's government. "Gay marriage is against the civil code and Aruban morals."

Though Aruba's gay marriage debate hinges on a dispute over law, differences in culture are a major factor. Despite strong ties to the Netherlands, Aruba shares more with Latin America than Europe. While Dutch is the official language, most Arubans speak Papiamento, a mix of Spanish and Portuguese. More than 80 percent of the island's 97,000 people are Catholic, and the largest number of immigrants come from nearby Venezuela and Colombia.

Same-Sex Marriage Rights Not Recognized

Few people are openly gay on the island, where locals say many homosexuals move to Holland rather than face persecution at home. "Being gay is still taboo in Aruba," said Guisette Croes, 41, a lesbian who owns a music store in the capital, Oranjestad. "You have Dutch law here, but you also have conservative Latin American people."

Charlene says she knew winning recognition of her marriage wouldn't be easy. Not having their marriage recognized meant Esther, a 38-year-old Dutch citizen, couldn't get health benefits from Charlene's job or stay on the island for more than six months a year under Aruban immigration laws. It also meant she wouldn't get custody of the couple's 2-year-old daughter should something happen to Charlene, who gave birth to the child with an implanted egg from Esther.

After filing their lawsuit, people began to heckle them and make critical remarks on the street, in the supermarket or at Charlene's job at the Aruban Department of Social Affairs. Walking downtown in the capital, Oranjestad, someone threw stones at them and their tires were slashed outside a hotel.

The couple received public support from Dutch gay rights groups and a liberal political party in the Netherlands, the D-66, but local organizations kept a much lower profile. The main Aruban gay rights organization declined to comment on the issue, saying they didn't want to draw unnecessary attention to their cause.

Charlene said that stress over their case caused her to have anxiety attacks, and in May she was fired from her government job after not returning from medical leave in Holland. She was put back on the payroll after threatening to sue.

Periodical Bibliography

The following articles have been selected to supplement the diverse views presented in this chapter.

The Economist	"No Wedding Bells; Australia," June 17, 2006.
The Economist	"Out of the Closet; Gay Rights in Latin America," March 10, 2007.
The Economist	"Until Death Do Us Part; Gay Rights," December 2, 2006.
Brodie Fenlon	"Do Same-Sex-Marriage Numbers Reflect Reality?" *The Globe and Mail* (Canada), September 13, 2007.
Jennifer Green	"Spain Legalizes Same-Sex Marriage," *The Washington Post*, July 1, 2005.
Wyndham Hartley	"Uneasy Marriage Between Creed and Constitution," *Business Day* (South Africa), November 29, 2006.
Ben Haywood	"Apocalypse Vow; Issues in the News: Same-Sex Marriage," *The Age* (Melbourne, Australia), May 26, 2008.
Tan Seow Hon	"Redefining Marriage: Where to Draw the Line?" *The Straits Times* (Singapore), July 30, 2007.
The Irish Times	"Debate on Validity of Same-Sex Marriages," November 10, 2006.
Lara Marlowe	"France's First Gay Marriage Set to Stay Annulled," *The Irish Times*, March 10, 2007.
Jesse McKinley	"California Ruling on Same-Sex Marriage Fuels a Battle, Rather Than Ending It," *The New York Times*, May 18, 2008.
UN Integrated Regional Information Networks	"South Africa; Same-Sex Marriage Bill Divides Opinion," November 16, 2006.

 **GLOBAL**VIEWPOINTS

Chapter

Marriage and Money

 **GLOBAL**VIEWPOINTS

CHAPTER

Marriage and Money

140

Many Middle Eastern and North African Men Cannot Afford to Marry

Navtej Singh Dhillon

In the following viewpoint, Navtej Singh Dhillon argues that the decline of marriages in the Middle East, especially in places such as Egypt and Iran, is because of potential grooms' lack of money. Dhillon notes the rising frustration of young men who are told not to engage in sexual activities outside marriage, yet are not given the opportunities in society to make enough money to afford to marry. According to Dhillon, this double bind interferes not only with one's feeling of self-worth, but also with social stance and even business opportunities. Dhillon is the director of the Middle East Youth Initiative at the Wolfensohn Center for Development.

As you read, consider the following questions:

1. According to Dhillon, what Middle Eastern country has the lowest percentage of men who marry by their late twenties?

2. As cited by the author, what is the percentage of youth unemployment in the Middle East?

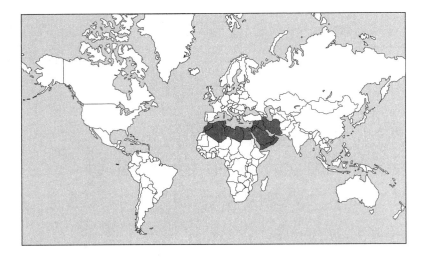

3. What two Middle Eastern countries are offering support or alternatives to traditional marriages, according to the author?

Hizbullah [an Islamic political and paramilitary organization based in Lebanon] may be calling protesters into the streets of Beirut. But Mazen Younes, a 26-year-old Lebanese marketing researcher, is more interested in getting married. Having a job that pays $2,000 a month—three times more than average—has a lot to do with it. That means, he says, "I may be able to marry before turning 30."

"Little more than a decade ago, 63 percent of Middle Eastern men married by their late 20s. Today the figure is just over 50 percent."

Contrast his situation with that of George Thabet, a 34-year-old Egyptian accountant who earns less than $300 a month—half of which goes to commuting costs. As an only son, he also has to support his aging parents. For him, matrimony is a frustratingly elusive dream.

Marriage, long the centerpiece of Middle Eastern life, is in crisis. The reason: A new generation of young men cannot afford to marry—a fact that's destined to exacerbate many of the region's social and political problems. Little more than a decade ago, 63 percent of Middle Eastern men married by their late 20s. Today the figure is just over 50 percent. Iran brings up the rear, at 38 percent, with the swathe of Maghreb between the Levant and Morocco only marginally better. Contrast that to Asia, which leads the nuptial race with 77 percent of men aged 25 to 29 being married, followed by 69 percent in Latin America and 66 percent in Africa.

The consequences of these trends are profound. In most Arab countries, a bachelor's life is devoid of economic and social opportunities. Marriage remains the path to adulthood, social status and legitimate sexual relationships. In contrast to Americans and Europeans, the majority of Arab men in their late 20s are not staying single by choice. They are forced into it by circumstances.

"Marriage is so critical to Egyptians, for example, that they spend some $3.8 billion annually on it."

Traditional Responsibilities and Modern Desires Make Marriage Unaffordable

Marriage is so critical to Egyptians, for example, that they spend some $3.8 billion annually on it. (That's more than the $2 billion in U.S. economic aid the country receives each year.) Most of these costs are borne by the groom—approximately $6,000 for a wedding, or four and a half times the average annual income. And while marriage costs have risen with inflation over the years, incomes have been largely stagnant since 1985. With youth unemployment exceeding 30 percent, growing numbers of young Middle Eastern men face serious financial obstacles to getting married, especially in early

---

Tajik Weddings Are Legally Downsized to Prevent Bankruptcy

In recent years, Tajikistan's president, Imomali Rahmon, has issued a number of decrees that regulate the daily life of his citizens, including bans on gold teeth, the use of cell phones in universities and big birthday parties.

He has also restricted people from holding extravagant weddings in an effort to stop Tajiks, 60 percent of whom live below the poverty line, from bankrupting themselves.

According to the new rules, weddings can't have more than 150 guests and can't last more than three hours. And, of course, the cooks are now allowed to make only one pot of plov [a traditional dish to serve at celebrations].

But here in Chertak, the groom's brother, Ilyas Kholov, says he likes the new law. The two brothers saved up for today's party by working on construction crews in Russia.

Kholov says he doesn't want to go into debt throwing a big wedding—that he would rather save money and spend it on a house.

Ivan Watson,
"Tajik Government Cracks Down on Wedding Size,"
All Things Considered, *National Public Radio, February 16, 2008.*

---

adulthood. Moroccan men nowadays marry at an average age of 32—seven years later than the previous generation.

Changing lifestyle expectations compound the problem. Few young people, these days, want to get married in traditional street tents. Dowries increasingly involve long lists of consumer goods. Newlyweds want homes of their own, instead of living with their parents. Western media dangles the good life before them, but most have no means of realizing it.

If the key to a stable Middle East is that children aren't worse off than their parents, then trouble is brewing. "The future in large part depends on the opportunities provided to young people, and at the moment we are nowhere close to solving this challenge," says Tarik Yousef, dean of the Dubai School of Government. Young men stranded between tradition and modernity tend toward volatility, radicalism and anger. They cannot afford to marry, yet religion and social custom bar sex outside marriage. They are expected to care for aging family members, yet can scarcely take care of themselves. Financial independence and marriage remain the mark of manhood and social standing, yet it is increasingly difficult to attain. In a part of the world where 60 percent of the population is under 25, this is a social time bomb.

The implications have not been lost on Middle East radicals. In Jordan, the Islamic Brotherhood offers free mass marriages and interest-free loans to young newlyweds. In Iran, President Mahmoud Ahmadinejad built his popularity by offering grants to young people getting married. In Egypt, the religious establishment is waging a war of morality against couples who take matters into their own hands by opting for urfi—a common-law marriage that sidesteps the costs of standard marriage and serves as a cover for premarital sex. Meanwhile, growing numbers of young men are opting out—literally—by emigrating to Europe or other countries where they hope to find jobs and build nest eggs. Most say they plan to return home, one day. Many never do.

For the most part, U.S. and European policy makers have ignored this marriage gap. And yet, it is one of the decisive trends shaping the region. "Those youths in the streets of Beirut are not just fighting for political change," says Mazen Younes. "They are asking about their own future."

India's Dowry Is Not a Gift

Neha Lalchandani

In the following viewpoint, Neha Lalchandani argues that the horrors of dowry exist in Indian marriages due, in large part, to a difficult distinction between gift and dowry and the high expectations of the groom's parents for compensation before the ceremony even commences. Lalchandani recognizes reasons why the dowry system was originally created and that people still give gifts according to tradition. Lalchandani points out that people avoid the term dowry—which has been outlawed—and rather give gifts to the bride and groom in celebration of their marriage. Lalchandani reports for The Times of India, *a daily Indian newspaper.*

As you read, consider the following questions:

1. According to Lalchandani, what are two reasons for the creation of the dowry system?

2. According to the author, why does advocate Mukta Gupta believe that dowry is a "catch-22 situation"?

3. According to Lalchandani, author Urvashi Butalia says, "There is nothing wrong with giving gifts to young people who are setting up homes." When does Butalia say gift giving and receiving become a problem?

Cases of girls getting space in boardrooms are not rare anymore. In fact, they have outsmarted boys in areas

Neha Lalchandani, "Blurred Line Between 'Gift' & Dowry," *The Times of India*, May 7, 2007. Reproduced by permission.

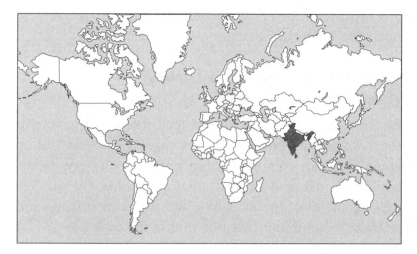

once thought to be men's stronghold. One would easily imagine then that girls are no longer a parent's burden when it comes to their marriage.

But, perhaps surprisingly, getting a daughter married is still a nightmare for many parents in India. Whatever the financial condition of the family, everyone wishes to accomplish their dream of marrying off their daughter in style.

The customary gifts exchanged—or rather given by the girl's family—ensures that most girls when they leave home for their husband's house are accompanied by suitcases overflowing with clothes, jewellery and, depending on the status of the girl's father, a vehicle.

In fact, few parents complain about the "giving" per se, even though giving dowry is also an offence. And trouble arises when demands go beyond what they can afford.

Nobody is quite sure how the dowry system started, but most agree that it was formulated to protect the girl financially in a society where the boy stood to inherit all property as a provision of stridhan [portion of the family's wealth belonging to women]. Another theory that floats is that the father, to take equal responsibility of the girl, would share a girl's expenses with her husband. The practice has obviously undergone numerous changes over the years.

A Wedding Gift Becomes Dowry When Greed Is Involved

The irony of the legal provision that states both giving and taking dowry are equally serious offences is that the only people who can complain about giving dowry are the very people who demand it. Said advocate Mukta Gupta: "It's a catch-22 situation for us. Giving dowry is an offence under the Dowry Prohibition Act but who is to come forward with the complaint?"

Nisha Sharma, who shot to fame in 2003 after she refused to marry Munish Dalal on the day of their marriage due to dowry harassment, said it is important to be clear on such issues rather than suffering later. "It was not an easy decision for me but if I had married him that day, my life could have been hell," she said.

"My daughter was waiting to enter the pandal [marquee] when her in-laws asked for a car and Rs 12.5 lakh [$25,000]. This was sheer blackmailing. My daughter took a stand then, but most parents would have bowed down to the pressure," said D D Sharma, Nisha's father.

"Parents are . . . caught off guard when demands come in at the last minute. Some parents are asked to cough up impossible amounts before the wedding ceremony can commence."

And there lies the catch. In several cases, parents are only too happy to comply with demands till they overshoot the amount originally decided. In the case of Mukta Chandolia, who was pushed down from the fifth floor of her house by her fiance, the fight started when her family was asked to give

An Expensive Demand

For most Indian parents the cost of a daughter's marriage is the single largest expense of their lives. In one rural sample the average cost of a daughter's marriage was six times the parents' annual income and, consequently, a cause of indebtedness and destitution. This expense is often labeled a "dowry."

The term dowry, however, has many different meanings: It is a gift made to cement bonds between two families—usually given in the form of jewelry or clothing. It is an investment to assist the newlyweds in setting up their homes—in the form of durable goods, or contributions toward a new business venture. It is a "pre-mortem" bequest to a daughter—enabling her to obtain a *stridhan* that she would not customarily be entitled to on the death of her father. It is a symbolic expense used to celebrate the marriage in an appropriate manner. And it is a "groomprice"—a transfer made to the groom's parents as an inducement to agree to the marriage. The academic and popular discourses on dowries both tend to confuse these different meanings, but they have extremely different implications for marital incentives, household bargaining, and the status of women.

Vijayendra Roa, "The Economics of Dowries in India," Oxford Companion to Economics, *ed. Kavshik Basu, Oxford: Oxford University Press, 2006.*

Rs 5 lakh more, besides the sum already agreed upon. "Dowry is an integral part of our system. I personally bought furniture for Deepak, Mukta's fiance, but the trouble started when he got too greedy," said Mukta's brother Manish. Obviously, there is something intrinsically wrong with our idea of marriage. Parents who praise their samdhis for not asking for dowry—

almost as if it is a favour being done—would on the other hand lavish them with clothes, gold, furniture, holiday packages and the works.

"This is not dowry. When my daughter gets married, I would like to give her gifts. This is the dream of each parent. And when I give gifts to my daughter, how can I not give something to her husband who is now like my son? This is the done thing in society and we have to live by its laws," says Vibha Arya (name changed).

"There is nothing wrong with giving gifts to young people who are setting up homes," says author Urvashi Butalia. "The problem is with the way the woman becomes the vehicle for the boy's family to acquire material goods and money," she adds. Parents are also caught off guard when demands come in at the last minute. Some parents are asked to cough up impossible amounts before the wedding ceremony can commence. "The education system seems to be a complete failure in this regard. How much you get in the wedding and how much you give is taken as an indication of your social status," says counsellor Sabhyata Arora.

Ireland's Marriage Rates Could Be Impacted by Prenuptial Agreements

The Sunday Business Post

In the following article, the author argues that recognizing prenuptial agreements may encourage Irish couples to marry by ensuring that their assets—from cars to family farms—are protected. In 2007, the Irish government began formally recognizing non-legally binding prenuptial agreements in divorce cases. This viewpoint exposes some arguments on the topic leading to this decision. The Sunday Business Post *is an Irish national Sunday newspaper first published in 1989.*

As you read, consider the following questions:

1. According to *The Sunday Business Post*, what is the problem with prenuptials as stated by "one leading London family law barrister"?

2. According to the article, how many Irish marriages end in divorce as compared to mainland Europe and America?

3. According to the article, what "advantages" does Senator Browne claim prenuptial agreements give?

Government proposals to consider legalizing prenuptial agreements could persuade more couples to marry.

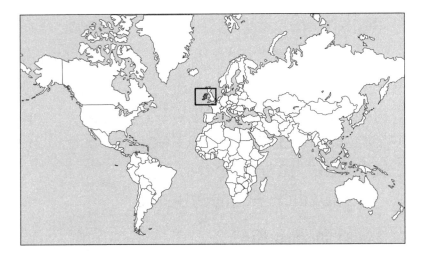

At present, one third of the children born in the state are born out of wedlock. This has significant implications for the rights of parents and their children in areas such as child custody, property rights, taxation and inheritance.

"Ireland and Britain are the only countries in the EU [European Union] which do not have legislation allowing 'prenups.'"

But many cohabiting couples choose not to marry because family law legislation does not permit them to agree in advance the distribution of their assets if they subsequently separate or divorce.

Prenuptial agreements are part of the family law system in many other common law countries, including the United States, Canada, New Zealand and Australia. Ireland and Britain are the only countries in the EU [European Union] which do not have legislation allowing 'prenups', though the family courts in Britain have begun taking such agreements into account during divorce cases.

Because of the in camera rule, it's not known what attitude Irish judges generally take to such agreements. But in the case of *RG v CG* in Galway last year, Ms Justice Mary Finlay Geoghegan quoted with approval the 2002 English decision in *X v X* in which Mr Justice Munby said: "A contract which purports to deprive the court of a jurisdiction which it would otherwise have is contrary to public policy."

Prenuptial Agreements Could Encourage Rise in Traditional Families in Ireland

Two years ago, the Solicitors Family Law Association (SFLA), which represents more than 5,000 solicitors in England and Wales, recommended to the British government that prenuptial agreements be made legally binding and enforceable, except where "significant injustice" might result.

The SFLA said that the demand for premarital agreements in Britain had increased because of:

- the higher number of second and subsequent marriages,

- media publicity about prenuptial agreements,

- the desire of couples to decide their own future, and

- the fear of failing to protect wealth.

The association said the enforceability of premarital contracts "might encourage more to choose marriage as an option for family life, especially when cohabitants have even greater uncertainty of outcomes". English solicitor Roger Bamber said: "For those who have been bitten once, the pre-marriage contract may be a way of ensuring that they are not twice shy."

The Relationship Between Legalizing Prenuptial Agreements and Marital Breakdown

But until now, the courts have held that such agreements are contrary to public policy because they undermine the institution of marriage by contemplating divorce. As one leading

London family law barrister put it: "The trouble with prenuptial agreements is that it's a bit like having a divorce before you get married." Prenuptial contracts are not enforceable in Ireland, but family law expert Geoffrey Shannon has called on the government to consider legalising such agreements in the context of its general review of marriage.

"We live in a sort of twilight zone at the moment, and people are entitled to certainty," he said. "Prenuptial agreements should be valid and enforceable, though the judiciary should retain a wide discretion to vary their terms."

Last week, Fine Gael [the United Ireland Party, a political party of the Republic of Ireland] Senator Fergal Browne tabled a private members' motion in the Seanad [upper house of Parliament] calling on the Law Reform Commission to examine the topic.

"The average age of a bride and groom has increased from being in the mid-20s in 1986 to being in their 30s in 2002," [Fine Gael Senator Fergal Browne] said. "It is not uncommon for a young couple who are marrying to have their own properties, which they have acquired, independent of their new spouse. We also have a considerable group of people in Ireland who are remarrying later in life."

"We cannot continue to ignore this aspect of marriage breakdown and divorce," said Browne. "A statement of assets prior to marriage could help to make things less messy afterwards if the relationship doesn't work out. However, it is important to consider all the aspects of legally recognising prenups, including the potential impact on the constitutional rights of women and children."

But Minister for Justice Michael McDowell said the Law Reform Commission was too busy to take on the review. Instead, he proposed that his department commission a study on the operation of the law in this area. In the course of the Seanad debate last Wednesday [October 2006], Browne said couples marrying nowadays tended to be older and better off.

"The average age of a bride and groom has increased from being in the mid-20s in 1986 to being in their 30s in 2002," he said. "It is not uncommon for a young couple who are marrying to have their own properties, which they have acquired, independent of their new spouse. We also have a considerable group of people in Ireland who are remarrying later in life."

However, the introduction of divorce in 1997 had led to an increasing incidence of marital breakdown.

"In Ireland, one in four marriages breakdown, compared to one in three on the European mainland and one in two in America," he said. "It is also worth noting that there is a high breakdown of marriage among newlyweds who have been together for less than two years."

Browne pointed out that, under European law, Irish couples could marry in other EU states where prenuptial agreements were allowed and he questioned whether a prenuptial agreement signed in, say, France would be enforceable here. "Unfortunately, we are in a twilight zone on that issue," he said.

Advantages of Prenuptial Agreements

Browne said he could see "great advantages in prenuptial agreements, particularly for people who are remarrying later in life and who have children from the first marriage. I believe it is logical that, ten years after the divorce referendum, where couples opt to have a prenuptial agreement, the state should recognise it and it should be taken into account in the case of a divorce or legal separation afterwards."

Browne said he did not believe that prenuptial agreements should be legally binding, because a couple's circumstances could change after marriage, but he said judges should be

---

Irish Farmers in Favor of Prenups

The majority of [Irish] farmers want their future spouse to sign a prenuptial agreement in an effort to safeguard the future of the farm, a major survey has revealed.

Two-thirds of those surveyed said farmers should insist upon prenuptial agreements.

The survey of more than 1,000 people was carried out at the Farming Independent stand over the three days of the Ploughing Championships.

Just 33 percent said farmers should not insist on prenuptial agreements.

The Irish Independent, *"Farmers Demand Prenups,"*
October 2, 2007. www.independent.ie. Reproduced by permission.

---

allowed to take such agreements into account, as they currently did with separation agreements.

"Prenuptials have the advantage of protecting many family businesses and family farms," he said. "Prenuptial agreements are also useful in cases where parents of children [who are getting married] may have helped them to purchase their house and their new spouse may not have contributed to the same extent. These cases are becoming more and more common as a result of the increasing unaffordabilty of housing, in particular for young people."

The senator said that a prenuptial agreement was "no different than someone taking out insurance on their car or taking out insurance on their home. Doing so does not mean you plan to damage either [of them]." He said that, if one took the view that prenuptials were unromantic, one could also argue that a person making a will early in life had a death wish.

Irish Courts May Take Prenuptial Agreements into Consideration

But McDowell said a prenuptial agreement might be motivated by one spouse's wish to avoid the application of family law provisions. "Whatever their motivation, prenuptial agreements have traditionally been held by the courts to be void on public policy grounds, on the basis that no contract envisaging the dissolution of a marriage should be enforceable," said McDowell.

"The removal of the constitutional prohibition on divorce in Ireland has weakened that public policy justification. However, the treatment of prenuptial agreements in Irish law must, nevertheless, still be considered in the context of the constitutional provisions relating to marriage."

McDowell said Irish courts could not grant a divorce unless proper provisions were made for both spouses and any children. "To the extent that a prenuptial agreement seeks to oust the jurisdiction of a court, it will fall foul of the constitutional requirement that the court must be satisfied that proper provision exists or will be made," he said.

The minister said that, while there was no explicit statutory requirement that a court should consider the terms of a prenuptial agreement in divorce proceedings, there was also no statutory bar to consideration.

"The terms of a prenuptial agreement may be . . . taken to indicate the intentions of the parties at the time of the making of the agreement," he said.

"As such, the terms of a prenuptial agreement may be considered by a court. However, the weight to be attached to such an agreement must be less than that attached to the factors which the court is, by statute, required to consider."

McDowell said the government accepted that there might be aspects of the law relating to prenuptial agreements that could be examined following the introduction of divorce. He said the government had agreed to commission a departmental study on the operation of the law and to bring forward recommendations for change where necessary.

Some Pakistani Women Are Sold into Marriage

Samar Minallah

In the following viewpoint, Samar Minallah argues that "sar paisa," the custom in which a man who wants to marry pays a family for their daughter, is common in some areas of the North-West Frontier Province of Pakistan. According to Minallah, the daughter is viewed as a product with a price to be bought and sold to the highest bidder; the higher the bride price, the more honor her family holds. Minallah points out that such a custom provokes violence within the community when a man cannot pay the full bride price, or when a woman runs from the system. Minallah reports for Newsline, *a biweekly Pakistani newsmagazine.*

As you read, consider the following questions:

1. According to Samar Minallah, why does a married woman have a higher market price than an unmarried woman in the sar paisa system?

2. According to the author, what happens to the man who does not pay compensation and to the wife involved?

3. According to the author, what is associated with "honor" in terms of sar paisa?

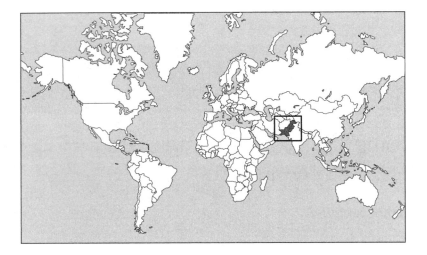

In some parts of NWFP [North-West Frontier Province of Pakistan], the custom of sar paisa is prevalent. The bride groom, in order to marry, pays a large sum of money to the girl's parents. This custom transforms her into an object of economic value, devoid of emotions or feelings. This living, breathing object of value can actually be sold and re-sold for a higher price—without a family's 'honour' being at stake. In fact, the higher her value, the more 'honour' her family gains.

Maimoona from Parachinar ended up in Kohat jail when she refused to be juggled from one man to another for a higher price. She was sold off to her cousin for 50,000 rupees [equivalent of approximately $1,246.57] in marriage. Meanwhile, her paternal cousin got an offer of one-and-a-half lakh rupees [equivalent of approximately $3,750], which he readily accepted on her behalf without her consent.

The only choice left before Maimoona was to escape with her husband. Having no written proof of their legal marriage, they ended up in Kohat jail. Maimoona's brothers and paternal cousins are trying their best to get her out of the jail in order to regain their lost honour and money.

An Abused Bride Escapes Her Home and Must Hide from the Law

Niyaz Khela, who is in her late fifties, belongs to Karak. She was sold off in marriage to a man much older to her. Still in her teens then, her husband would often beat her over trivial matters. In order to escape from a life of misery, she eloped with another man whom she had met while she had gone to fetch water.

Having to choose between the probability of being killed and living a life of torment with a man who would continue to mistreat her, Niyaz Khela chose the former.

Barefoot, with no material possession, she, along with her paramour, hid in the crevices of the rugged mountains of Karak, dodging the killers that chased her. "The gunshots did not scare me because I preferred death to going back to an abusive husband," says Niyaz Khela. However, after two years of hiding, Niyaz Khela's second husband managed to pay 10,000 rupees to her ex-husband, which was double the amount initially paid by the first husband as 'bride price.' This way not only was his pride elated but his lost 'honour' was also regained in the form of financial profit.

Bride Price Compensation

In Karak, a married woman has a higher price in the market because her ex-husband, if alive, has to be compensated for his financial loss. Unless, he is given a higher price than what he had initially paid for the woman, he receives pighore (taunt) from the community.

If money is not paid as compensation, the male perpetrator is usually killed and the woman sent back to the parents, who try once again to marry her off. The money they receive from her second marriage is paid off to her aggrieved ex-husband.

Thus, here, more men are killed in such offences because a woman, even if she is divorced or abandoned by the husband,

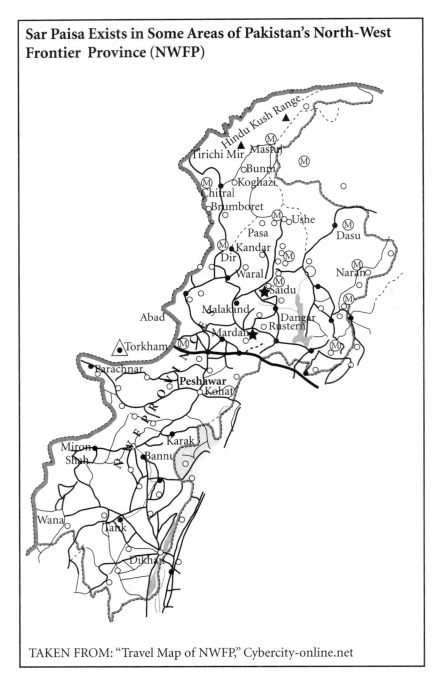

Sar Paisa Exists in Some Areas of Pakistan's North-West Frontier Province (NWFP)

TAKEN FROM: "Travel Map of NWFP," Cybercity-online.net

still has a price in the market. The man can also be acquitted if he pays a huge amount of money as compensation to the aggrieved party. Therefore honour, in this context, is linked more to wealth than to one's moral behaviour.

The High Price of Honour

As Niyaz Khela confirms, 'Moozh watan kay topak aao paisa balaa dee,' (In our village guns and money are giants!). It's been more than four decades since Niyaz Khela abandoned her village and settled in Islamabad as an economic migrant. Her second husband left her for another woman whom he bought at a reasonable price.

Living in a small ghetto, practicing her customs in a foreign land, Niyaz Khela had to work hard to marry off her three children, all on her own. She worked as a labourer, making bricks for the high-rise buildings of Islamabad to pay for a bride for one of her sons. For her younger son, she got a bride in swarra (exchange of women) as an exchange with her own daughter.

It is interesting that while honour can be tarnished with a slight slip of behaviour, customs like swarra and sar paisa, where a woman is used as an object of value or an instrument of building alliances, bring honour. Niyaz Khela, like many other Pukhtuns, has no choice but to follow the customs her forefathers practiced. If a Pakhtun fails to act according to Pakhtunwali, he/she is no longer considered a dhroon Pakhtun (an honourable Pakhtun). It is very hard even for a very gallant Pakhtun to face the venomous pighore [taunt]. The only way to free oneself from the wrath of pighore is to prove his/her allegiance to 'Pakhunwali' (the Pakhtun code of conduct), which could even be at the price of someone's life.

In Japan, a Tokyo Businessman Revolutionizes Weddings

John Dodd

In the following viewpoint, John Dodd points out that Masahiro Hirose revolutionized the wedding industry in Japan through his company, Bridal Hirose, by challenging the Japanese norm of getting married. According to Dodd, Hirose offers choices to modern brides and grooms, such as having a wedding in a more intimate setting like a restaurant, private home, or park, instead of settling on what was a Japanese marriage monopoly: the hotel package wedding. Dodd also recognizes Hirose's newest and most innovative addition to Japan's wedding industry: the "anniversary wedding." Dodd writes for Japan Inc., *a Japanese business magazine that covers such interests as technology, education, politics, real estate, and other Japanese industries.*

As you read, consider the following questions:

1. According to Dodd, what was the average amount a Japanese bride's father would spend on a wedding before Hirose introduced different choices of marriage celebrations to Japan's wedding industry?
2. According to the author, what is a "teitaku wedding"?
3. According to the author, how has Hirose approximately "tripled the size of the Japanese wedding market"?

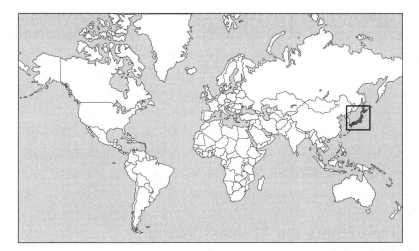

Tokyo businessman Masahiro Hirose is a bit of a maverick. He runs one of Japan's most innovative wedding planning and production agencies, yet secretly he yearns to be a politician.

So far his ambitions have been frustrated by his success in business, but, ironically, his search for the competitive edge is now bringing him closer to politics in local government. His present goal is to introduce a radical new trend in Japanese weddings—involving public park space and lots and lots of guests.

Hirose has always been interested in politics and the mass communication of ideas and concepts. As a high school student he learned from history books that the charismatic individuals who were the forerunners of today's politicians have brought about great changes. Then later as a junior at Hosei University he joined the Shinjiyu Club, a politics study group, and got to hear such speakers as [politician] Kakuei Tanaka expound on financial issues. He also got involved in the debating club and did a lot of speechmaking. In fact he enjoyed university so much that it took him six years to complete a four-year course. His father finally had enough after the fourth year and warned him that he'd better graduate then find something useful to do.

Hirose's answer to Dad's threat was typically independent. He took charge of his own finances, continued his studies, and put himself through the last two years of school by holding down a variety of part-time jobs as well as studying. He worked on an evening railroad gang in the Tokyo subways, delivered newspapers on-campus, and later was employed as a short-order cook at a beef bowl (gyudon-ya) chain. If nothing else, he learned from slaving in a hot kitchen that there had to be a better way in life. He also learned that hard work is the way out of poverty.

Hirose Enters the Business World in Preparation to Own a Company

After graduation from college, Hirose was preparing to take the next step in fulfilling his dream to be a politician by becoming an assistant for a Diet member [the National Diet of Japan is Japan's legislature]. Then a friend pointed out that in order to represent the people, he first had to experience the life of the people. Hirose recalls later, "Maybe this friend realized that I didn't have the brain power to think on my feet!" In any case, the logic struck a chord in the young Hirose and he promptly joined a small securities company. His rationale was that his new employer, Tokyo Securities Ltd., would allow him to study the inner workings of capitalism and just how finance helped Japan stay strong.

While learning about the mechanics of finance, Hirose kept his hopes of being a politician alive by honing his public speaking skills. He chose an unusual way to do it, by moonlighting on weekends, acting as a Master of Ceremonies [MC] at the weddings of friends, then later MC-ing on a professional basis. Again, Hirose's choice of the high road meant he worked 365 days a year. But the financial and professional rewards kept him at it.

As Hirose gained experience, he outgrew the small firm he originally joined, and entered Merrill Lynch. This was his first experience with an international finance firm and he embarked on an intensive period of learning just how finance and political events are tied together. Thanks to his outgoing personality and can-do attitude, he also got roped into some of Merrill's more difficult real estate negotiations, and had some experiences with Japan's underworld that he would rather forget. Hirose laughs, "Merrill Lynch was a good experience for me, but I never did learn to speak English well. Luckily I was a pretty good negotiator, so even in the depth of the recession in the mid-nineties, I was still of value to the company."

However, after twelve stressful years in the securities industry, and specifically after a particular run-in with a Yakuza-related company, Hirose started to question his choice of career and his earlier dreams were rekindled. He knew that he would need time of his own to further any political ambitions, and decided the best way to do this was to run a company of his own. He established his company, Bridal Hirose, in December 1993 at the age of thirty-six.

Hirose Recognizes a Gap in the Japanese Wedding Market

It was only natural that he would pick the industry that he'd been moonlighting in all these years, but in true maverick fashion, he wanted to shake up the conservative players. His radical idea was to give customers the freedom of choice to decide programs for their own weddings.

To understand why Hirose's concept was radical, we need to consider conditions back in 1994, when the burst of the bubble wreaked financial and psychological havoc in Japan. Back then, most weddings were held according to a set formula in downtown city hotels. Weddings were less a celebration of union and more a rite of passage—especially for the bride's father, who was being saddled with an average wedding cost of [yen] 10 million.

At the time the standard wedding consisted of a series of mini "rites" developed by the hotel industry over the previous thirty years. The couple would be offered a basic program, then some add-on services to boost revenue. Needless to say, the hotels in particular would prey on the bride-to-be's concern about getting everything just right, and slip in extra services to make her feel that her wedding was more complete. Couples who wanted the flexibility to add dancing or music played by friends were turned away by the hotels.

But what Hirose could see, if only because his financial background had taught him to observe trends, was that the wedding industry was in decline. He realized that the baby boomers would peak in 1996 and 1997. There were on average 1 million weddings a year in that period, and in 2003 just 740,000 couples wed in Japan. If the trend continues, then in twenty years time, there will be just 450,000 marriages in Japan. This has been tough on the hotels. For example, the Hotel Okura, which once managed an average of two weddings a day, now manages just one. Clearly this is a major challenge for the industry.

"Hirose . . . predicted that as the financial and personal independence of young women increased, so too would the desire to marry on their own terms."

Some hotels tried to combat the downturn in the wedding trade by hosting up-market funerals—naturally following the nation's demographics. But, as Hirose explains, a hotel that goes into the funeral reception business is nailing its own coffin for one simple reason: the reception room starts to reek of incense, and odor-sensitive female guests realize what it was used for. "No one wants to celebrate a happy occasion in a room previously used for a sad one," says Hirose.

Hirose also predicted that as the financial and personal independence of young women increased, so too would the desire to marry on their own terms. Or, not get married at all. As Hirose says, "If you're a professional working woman in your mid- to late-twenties and you're making 6 to 8 million yen a year, why would you want to tie up with a salaried worker making just 5 million yen a year, get married, stop working, and have a family? It just doesn't make financial sense." So a lot of women put off getting married.

Hirose Introduces Choice into Japan's Wedding Industry

So, with these two trends in mind, Hirose pioneered customized weddings, helping couples share their joy with friends and family in a way that would be remembered for the rest of their lives. In creating a memorable experience, he frequently clashed with hotel rules and regulations and in frustration turned to clubs and restaurants for venues and flexibility. He found that the recession was causing restaurateurs a lot of hardship, and his approaches were well received. Now not only could he offer customers their own program, but in some cases a lot better food as well—and all at a reasonable price.

Hirose was able to provide a range of production services to help out first-timers. To the fastidious Japanese, these services range from the obvious tasks of venue and food through to choice of politically correct seating arrangements, wording and format of invitations, and even printing parking maps for guests in space-challenged Tokyo. For a while the new trend helped Bridal Hirose grow by more than 30 percent a year, but in 1999–2000, the market for restaurant weddings peaked, and Hirose was busy planning the next big thing.

The next big thing was the "teitaku wedding," a casual wedding in a gracious private home rented for the occasion. The concept arose in Europe and America, from where more and more young Japanese women were returning after overseas study. One problem in Japan, however, is that there are few spacious private homes, let alone those for rent, and thus the concept was pulled back to the hotels, and right now these casual events are enjoying a mini boom. The teitaku wedding is, of course, for wealthier couples, and there are only three hotels in Tokyo tony enough to fit the bill: the Okura, the Imperial, and the New Otani.

"Hirose needs to keep innovating, and his latest spin is a concept called 'park weddings.' Again, looking to the West for inspiration, Hirose reckons that in Western Europe and the United States up to 40 percent of weddings are now being held in parks and other open spaces. He was especially inspired by weddings in Central Park in New York City."

The quintessential teitaku wedding involves a garden ceremony, dinner inside, then a return to the garden for dessert and drinks—all, of course, in the middle of downtown Tokyo. Hirose says that about 70 percent of these weddings have between 150 and 160 guests, with some of the more extravagant ones running to 250 people. A typical teitaku wedding runs the bride's father around 3 to 4 million yen, but since it is tradition for guests to give gifts of money the overall cost is halved.

Business being what it is, Hirose needs to keep innovating, and his latest spin is a concept called "park weddings." Again, looking to the West for inspiration, Hirose reckons that in Western Europe and the United States up to 40 percent of weddings are now being held in parks and other open spaces. He was especially inspired by weddings in Central Park in New York City. Certainly this is the case in areas with clement weather, including California, Hawaii, and the U.S. southwest. Now Hirose wants to bring park weddings to Japan—but not just any park. Given that he has been moving up the value chain, with the teitaku productions at brand-name hotels, his

---

Survey of Trends in Japanese Marriage

Nearly 90 percent of single Japanese men and women in their twenties and thirties hope to marry someday, with motivations including love, the wish to create a home, and the desire to have children. The most important criteria by which these people judge prospective marriage partners are character, shared values, and compatibility. They see the ideal couple as equal partners who talk a lot and can discuss anything. However, one in three singles does not wish to have a wedding ceremony, while nearly 70 percent want only one or two children, and 15 percent do not want any children at all. With people tending to marry later nowadays and a growing number of people choosing not to marry at all, the number of children is on the decrease.

Trends in Japan, *"What Is the Ideal Marriage?"*
April 30, 2003. http://web-japan.org.

---

plan is to focus on downtown parks and public spaces. What especially caught his eye was the Tokyo City government's decision to rent out Hibiya Park for events. Hirose was the first to approach the government with a wedding concept. They liked it, and awarded him the rights to conduct weddings during [fiscal year] FY2005, beginning April 2005.

Anniversary Weddings

However, the contract is both a blessing and burden. To start with, he only has six months to create a new trend. While he is confident that his recent marketing and PR [public relations] efforts will generate business leads, he is hedging his bets with another concept—the "anniversary wedding." The idea is for Japanese older couples to have a Western-style wedding decades after their first one, which may have been cut price.

> *"I think people will start to realize that as a social institution, marriage needs to be reaffirmed in a social setting. These events will help stressed couples to remind themselves what their real values should be."*

The great thing about these re-weddings is that they can be a lot more casual and are more for the re-bride to enjoy wearing white and getting together with her friends in a festive atmosphere; thus they are ideally suited for a pavilion in a park. Furthermore, it is acceptable for two or three couples to re-tie the knot at the same wedding, thus reducing costs and adding to the festive atmosphere. Hirose is trying to get multiple generations of families to re-wed all together: that is, the grandparents, the parents, and the first-time groom and bride.

Actually, Hirose is making good progress in marketing the "anniversary wedding" concept. "What, with all the divorce and difficulties married couples have these days," he says, "it's really tough on the kids. I want to promote the anniversary weddings as a means for couples to renew their marriage vows in front of their families and friends, and to renew their relationships. I think people will start to realize that as a social institution, marriage needs to be reaffirmed in a social setting. These events will help stressed married couples to remind themselves what their real values should be." That's a good pitch. And considering that there could be silver, gold, and diamond anniversary celebrations, he may have just tripled the size of the Japanese wedding market.

Already, Hirose has organized an anniversary wedding at the Hibiya Park location . . . the event was a great success—with three unrelated couples in their 40s, 50s, and 60s reaffirming their vows during the course of a summer's afternoon, and with over 1,000 friends and family members in attendance. Many in the industry have been amazed to see just how many people turned out—and the atmosphere was more like a music concert than a private party. Needless to say, the event received wide media coverage. His next event was at Ark Hills on November 22, 2004—an important date, as 1-1-2-2 can be read as "li fufu," meaning "a nice couple." As they say, never underestimate the power of a driven entrepreneur to create concepts and change.

At forty-eight years of age, Hirose has become known as the father of wedding planners. This is because after several years of doing business he realized that the only way to break the hold of the hotels was to create market momentum through education. So in 1996, he started a training school for planners and producers. It was a hit, and in the last eight years he has had hundreds of people graduate from the course. Naturally, education is a two-edged sword, and while his pupils have indeed gone on to change the industry, a number of them have been sufficiently successful to become competitors. Hirose takes it all in stride and says that providing the industry keeps moving weddings up market—something that is likely to continue so long as women keep putting off the marriage date—then there is enough for all the players.

Periodical Bibliography

The following articles have been selected to supplement the diverse views presented in this chapter.

Jennifer Conlin	"'To Have and to Hold ... All the Cash I Can'; In the Wake of Two British Court Rulings on Divorce, Marriage Has Become a High-Stakes Gamble," *The International Herald Tribune*, February 10, 2007.
M.P. Dunleavey	"When Money and Marriage Collide," *The New York Times*, April 21, 2007.
The East African Standard	"Kenya; Dowry—Does It Put a Price On Women?" February 24, 2007.
Raina Kelley	"Expert Advice: Love by the Numbers; Your New Marriage is Bliss—Until the Bickering over Finances Begins. How to Keep Money from Wrecking Your Home Life," *Newsweek*, April 9, 2007.
New Vision	"Uganda; Love, Money or Both?" October 5, 2007.
New Vision	"Uganda; Where a Bride Dictates Her Price," May 3, 2007.
Lisa Shidler	"Health-Benefits Tax Bill Draws Adviser Interest; All Types of Couples Would Receive a Spousal Break," *Investment News*, April 9, 2007.
Linda Stern	"When She Makes More than Him; It Can Make a Difference in a Marriage. Spouses Must Learn to Enjoy the Money, Share Responsibilities and Accept the Costs," *The Gazette* (Montreal, Canada), May 5, 2007.
Sarah Treleaven	"Not Tonight, Dear, I'm Overdrawn; Fights Over Finances," *National Post* (Canada), February 21, 2008.
Vanguard (Lagos, Nigeria)	"Nigeria; Far from the Altar," March 6, 2008.

GLOBAL VIEWPOINTS

CHAPTER 5

Marriage and Sex

Worldwide Study Shows Married Couples Have More Sex than Singles

Jennifer Harper

In the following viewpoint, Jennifer Harper points out that a worldwide study involving over a million people from fifty-nine countries sheds light on the fact that married people have more sex than single people, correcting the stereotype that marriage slows sexual activity. Harper also debunks such preconceived notions as sex becoming more frequent among young people and the assumption that many people have multiple sex partners. Jennifer Harper is a writer for The Washington Times, *a U.S. daily newspaper known for its investigative reporting.*

As you read, consider the following questions:

1. According to the survey cited by Harper, what percentage of married American couples claim to have had sex within the previous month of responding to the survey?

2. According to the author, in what countries do the most sexually active married people live?

3. The author points out that the lowest median age at which young men have sex for the first time is sixteen, and for young women, is fifteen. From what countries are these statistics for young men and women associated?

Swinging singles rule? The gospel according to supermarket magazines and cheesy primetime TV has met its match.

The world's first true study of global sexual health revealed yesterday that married people are having more sex than their single peers. Mr. and Mrs. are just fine in the bedroom, said British researchers who investigated the sexual mores of more than 1 million people in 59 countries.

Married People Engage in Sex More Frequently than Single People

Among Americans, more than 90 percent of married couples reported that they had sex in the previous month, compared with just over 50 percent among single men and women. The findings were similar in France, Britain and other industrialized nations, though British and French singles fared the best in the bunch, with more than 60 percent of singles reporting some recent luck in the bedroom.

There were a few highs and lows. The least sexually active married couples were found in some African countries, with less than 50 percent reporting that they had sex recently. The most active marrieds, in order, were found in France, Kazakhstan, Rwanda, the United States, Britain and Australia.

"'Monogamy is the dominant pattern everywhere. . . . Most people are married, and married people have the most sex.'"

"We did have some of our preconceptions dashed," said Kaye Wellings, a professor of sexual health at the University of London's School of Hygiene and Tropical Medicine. She based her conclusions on an analysis of 161 medical, social science and public health studies that were completed in the past 10 years.

American Sex Survey Evaluates the Sex Lives of Married Couples

	Married <3 years	Married >10 years
Have sex at least several times a week	72%	32%
Sex life very exciting	58%	29%
Enjoy sex a great deal	87%	70%

TAKEN FROM: Analysis by Gary Langer, with Cheryl Arnedt and Dalia Sussman, "Poll: American Sex Survey," *ABC News*, October 21, 2004.

"Monogamy is the dominant pattern everywhere. . . . Most people are married, and married people have the most sex," she wrote in the study, published in the *Lancet*, a British medical journal.

Increase in Youth Sex and Multiple Sex Partners Are Not Common

What's more, folks aren't engaging in sex at ever-earlier ages as some provocative culture mavens, performers or clothing manufacturers might want us to think. Though there are regional variances, sexual activity begins for most men and women "in the late teen years," the study found.

The median age for first sexual intercourse in the United States is just over 17 for young men and almost 18 for young women, about average on the global stage. The lowest median age for losing virginity among men was about 16 in both Peru and Britain. For women, it was 15 in several African nations, though many of those nations also reported the average age to marry among women ranged from 15 to 17.

Although marketers may foster a reputation of racy young Americans, the percentage of youths who had sex before 15 in the United States has dropped in the past three decades, from about 20 percent in 1975 to about 15 percent today.

"People who fear a tide of youthful promiscuity might take heart in the fact that trends toward early and premarital sex are neither as pronounced or prevalent as is sometimes assumed," the study said.

The so-called swinging life replete with multiple sex partners appears to be a myth, it found.

"Most people report having only one recent sexual partner," the study said, though the phenomenon was more common among men than women on a worldwide basis. In addition, men and women who reported having more than one partner lived in industrialized nations rather than developing ones.

Irish Opinions of Sex Have Liberalized over the Past Thirty Years

Eithne Donnellan

In the following viewpoint, Eithne Donnellan argues that there has been significant change in the Irish perception of sex over the past thirty years, especially in terms of premarital sex. Donnellan asserts that overall Irish attitudes toward sex have become more liberal over time, as observed in the first major survey of sexual health and relationships conducted in the Republic of Ireland in 2006. The survey asked approximately seven thousand five hundred people, between the ages of eighteen and sixty-four, about such issues as sex education, premarital sex, one-night stands, homosexuality, and knowledge of sexually transmitted diseases, female fertility, and contraceptives. Donnellan is a writer for The Irish Times, *a daily Irish newspaper published in Dublin since the 1850s.*

As you read, consider the following questions:

1. According to the survey to which Donnellan refers, what percentage of Irish people thought premarital sex was always wrong in 1973?

2. According to the author, what percentage of Irish people reported being taught sex education at home?

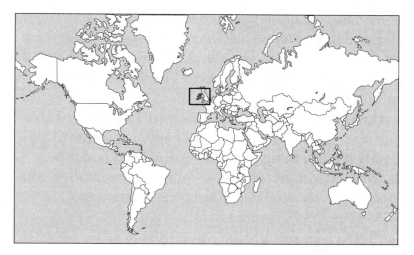

3. What form of contraception does the author say is used as commonly as the birth control pill among married Irish people?

There has been a dramatic change in the attitude of Irish people to a range of sexual behaviours, including sex before marriage, over the past three decades, according to new research.

The first large-scale study of sexual health and relationships in the State, published yesterday [October 16, 2006], found just 6 percent of people now think premarital sex is always wrong, compared to 71 percent of people back in 1973.

The survey of almost 7,500 people, aged 18 to 64 years, was commissioned by the Department of Health and the Crisis Pregnancy Agency and carried out by the ESRI [the Economic and Social Research Institute] and the Royal College of Surgeons in Ireland.

Sex Education

It shows that over time people have also become more accepting of sex education in schools. At least 92 percent of those surveyed supported sex education for young people on the subjects of sexual intercourse, sexual feelings, contraception, safer sex and homosexuality. Approximately 90 percent of people who supported sex education favoured it being taught in school and around 80 percent believed it should be provided in the home.

However, the Irish Study of Sexual Health and Relationships found that 44 percent of people had received no sex education at all, but most under 35s had received some.

Of those who received some form of sex education, just 29 percent reported receiving it at home. A minority found talking to either parent about sex easy.

Liberal Attitudes Among Young Adults

The research shows 40 percent of the population consider one-night stands to be "always wrong". Among the other 60 percent, 16 percent felt they are never wrong, 30 percent believe they are sometimes wrong and 14 percent believe they are mostly wrong.

The survey also confirms that attitudes to homosexuality in Ireland "have significantly softened in recent decades". It found the proportion of under 25 year olds who hold the view that same-sex relationships are never justified decreased by 66 percent between 1981 and 2005. The proportion of those aged 55 to 64 with the same attitude decreased by 40 percent over the same period. "This suggests that liberalisation has been most pronounced among younger Irish people," the report said.

Knowledge of STDs and Female Fertility

The study also looked at issues like knowledge levels about risk of sexually transmitted diseases [STDs] like HIV by asking three basic questions about the condition. About 30 percent of the population got at least one answer wrong. "It is worrying that over two-fifths of men and around half of women with primary education alone do not have accurate knowledge about the risks of HIV," the report stated.

It also expressed concern that levels of knowledge about female fertility in Ireland "are poor" and falling. Just 31 percent of men and 56 percent of women could identify the time at which a woman is most fertile—half way between periods.

Contraception

On issues around contraception some 32 percent of women said the cost of the contraceptive pill would discourage them from using it and 15 percent of the whole cohort said the cost of condoms would discourage their use.

The research found that among those using contraception the most common forms are condoms and the contraceptive pill. "Among married people, sterilisation is almost as common as use of the pill," it said.

Among those who did not use contraception, the most common reason cited was being postmenopausal. But among younger age groups, the most commonly cited reason was drinking alcohol or taking drugs.

And some 14 percent of those having sex for the first time with a partner they had just met said they did not use a condom because "they trusted" their partner would not have a sexually transmitted disease.

"52 percent of men and 42 percent of women think the morning-after pill should be available without prescription."

Same-Sex Relationships

Overall some 2.7 percent of men and 1.2 percent of women identified themselves as homosexual or bisexual, but 7.1 percent of men and 4.7 percent of women reported a homosexual experience at some time in their life so far.

The study also established that most men who currently have sex with men have a similar number of partners as het-

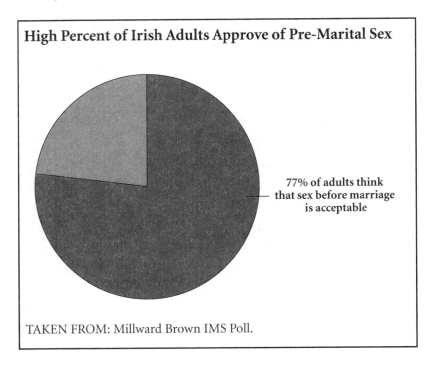

High Percent of Irish Adults Approve of Pre-Marital Sex

77% of adults think that sex before marriage is acceptable

TAKEN FROM: Millward Brown IMS Poll.

erosexual men, but women with homosexual experience tend to have lower numbers of partners than the general female population.

Sexual Health Survey: Main Points

- Most people believe young people today should receive sex education in school and in the home.

- Only 6 percent of the population now think sex before marriage is always wrong.

- Just 40 percent of Irish people consider one-night stands to be always wrong.

- Some 64 percent of the population believe abortion is acceptable in at least some circumstances.

- 52 percent of men and 42 percent of women think the morning-after pill should be available without prescription.

- 6.4 percent of men say they have paid for sex at some stage in their life.

- The age at which men first have sex has fallen by five years in the past four decades. The age at which women first have sex has fallen by six years. The median age at which under-25s now have sex is 17 years.

- Some 2.7 percent of men and 1.2 percent of women in the State identify themselves as homosexual or bisexual.

- Cost of contraception would discourage some from using it.

Japanese Sexless Marriages Are Responsible for Japan's Population Decline

Deborah Cameron

In the following viewpoint, Deborah Cameron argues that the trend of sexless marriages in Japan has resulted in fewer births every year, ultimately slowing the Japanese population rate. Cameron refers to a survey of six hundred Japanese wives, another survey of sixteen hundred wives, and a survey of one thousand men to acknowledge the lack of sex in Japanese marriages. Cameron points out that although Japan exudes a sexual culture, it is often lacking between husband and wife. Cameron is a writer for The Age, *an Australian daily newspaper first published in 1854 in Melbourne, Australia.*

As you read, consider the following questions:

1. According to the survey of sixteen hundred wives to which Cameron refers, what percentage of Japanese marriages are sexless?

2. According to the *Asahi Shimbun* survey, what percentage of Japanese men said they "no longer even saw their wives as women"?

3. According to the author, demographers predict that Japan' population will decline by how much by 2050?

Deborah Cameron, "A Nation Where Marriage Beds Have Gone Cold," *The Age*, February 5, 2005. Copyright © 2005 The Age Company Ltd. Reproduced by permission of the publisher and the author.

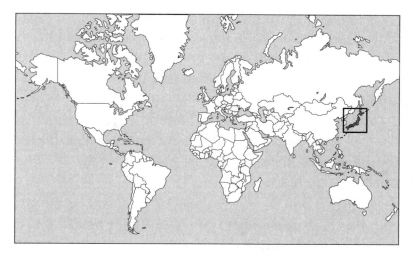

Bonus season has a double meaning for at least one frustrated Japanese salary man. He gets lucky at the office and when he delivers the cheque, a little spark is put back into his otherwise sexless marriage.

As part of a deal to prop up their relationship, the man and his 36-year-old wife agreed to have sex only twice a year at bonus time. But before the money was even in the bank, she had second thoughts.

"I have told my husband that I want to divorce him because I don't want to have sex," his wife told a newspaper survey.

"I compromised after his counterproposal to have sex only twice a year in bonus season. But I feel blue when a bonus season is coming."

Lack of Sexual Attraction Between Husbands and Wives Raises Questions

Theirs officially is a "sexless marriage". It is a growing trend in Japan, identified in several surveys and books, and has become a national concern as the country searches for the reasons behind its collapsing birthrate and looming steep population decline.

Of 600 wives surveyed by one of Japan's biggest newspaper groups, *Asahi Shimbun*, 26 percent said that they had not had sex with their husbands in the previous 12 months. An earlier survey of 1600 wives was bleaker still, putting more than 45 percent of marriages into the sexless category.

Husbands too are turned off. In a survey of 1000 men done late last year, almost 40 percent reported that they had not had sex with their wives at all in the previous six months or had done so just once.

Compared with a survey done 10 years ago, when just 5 percent of husbands said they were sexless, it points to severe relationship problems. Sexlessness is defined by the Japan Society of Sexual Science as "no sexual contact between a married couple for more than one month".

It is a remarkable picture full of contradictions. At first sight, Japan, and particularly its capital, is vibrant and hedonist. Young couples are acutely aware of their sexuality, Internet matchmaking sites are overrun with married and unmarried candidates, affairs are common, the love hotels do an open and uninhibited trade, and sexually explicit material is published in mainstream comics.

"The sexless marriage is a small but intriguing part of what is behind Japan's collapsing birth rate, which at 1.29 births per 1,000, is one of the lowest in the world."

And yet when it's time for couples to get serious and have families, they freeze. Many couples in the surveys said that after their first child was born, desire vanished.

Almost 20 percent of men in the *Asahi Shimbun* survey said that they no longer even saw their wives as women.

"We are sort of roommates rather than a married couple," according to a 31-year-old information technology engineer who said that he had not had sex with his wife for two years.

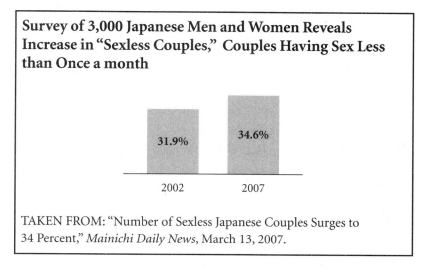

Survey of 3,000 Japanese Men and Women Reveals Increase in "Sexless Couples," Couples Having Sex Less than Once a month

31.9%	34.6%
2002	2007

TAKEN FROM: "Number of Sexless Japanese Couples Surges to 34 Percent," *Mainichi Daily News*, March 13, 2007.

He claimed that it was because she had gained weight after becoming keen on computer games when they married four years ago. Husbands with almost non-existent sex lives said things fell apart within five years of marriage.

Population Plummet

The sexless marriage is a small but intriguing part of what is behind Japan's collapsing birth rate, which at 1.29 births per 1000, is one of the lowest in the world.

While policy makers discuss making child care more available and doing more to support families, it may be that the problem is much more fundamental. No sex, no babies.

A population crunch is just around the corner. After an expected peak in 2006, demographers predict a 25 percent population decline by 2050. Coupled with growing numbers of people over the age of 65, indeed over the age of 100, it is an outcome that spells the end of Japan as we know it.

Ugandan Adultery Has Been Decriminalized

Percy Night Tuhaise

In the following viewpoint, Percy Night Tuhaise, a writer for
New Vision *argues in favor of a Ugandan court ruling that de-
criminalizes adultery while keeping it illegal, recognizing that the
criminal adultery laws that previously existed only protected
married men, not women. Thus, on the basis of gender discrimination, the Constitutional Court deemed the law unconstitutional. However, the author describes the social conditioning that
still divides gender roles in Uganda as a hindrance to the purpose of decriminalizing adultery, as well as the misunderstand-
ing that because adultery is not a criminal offense, it is not
wrong.* New Vision *is a major Ugandan daily newspaper.*

As you read, consider the following questions:

1. According to the author, what have gender scholars
   claimed the original criminal adultery laws were created
   to do?

2. According to the author, what is one example of the
   treatment of women in Uganda's patriarchal society?

3. What is one religious or social justification some Ugan-
   dans believe is a reason for criminalizing adultery?

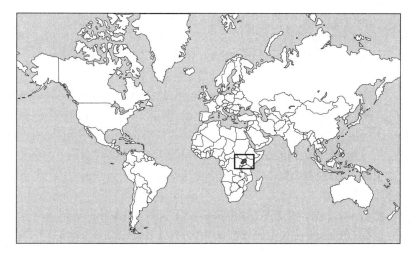

The [2007] Constitutional Court ruling which decriminalised adultery was long overdue. The criminal adultery laws were protecting the married male, in the typical patriarchal fashion. From the wording of Section 154 of the Penal Code Act, men were given more sexual freedom than women.

A married man could go "on rampage" with any unmarried woman for as long as he was not "tampering" with another man's wife.

However, the married wife was not supposed to go on any "rampage" at all, not even with an unmarried man! What hypocrisy! As if that was not enough, it was only the "aggrieved" married male (husband of the adulterous wife) who qualified for the compensation. . . . The married wife of an adulterous husband was not entitled to any compensation, that is, such a wife would not be "aggrieved"!

Double Standards

This is a reflection of the double standards of patriarchal society.

It presupposes that men have proprietory rights over women's bodies. Gender scholars have argued that this was engineered to ensure or guarantee that all children in the marriage belong to the man for inheritance matters, or to ensure that there is certainty in issues of paternity so that property rightfully flows along the paternal line from man to his offsprings.

This was in addition to ensuring that a married woman only has sexual relations with her husband though the husband could "wander" among unmarried women. This patriarchal trait of double standards permeates many other areas of law like property laws, marriage laws, divorce laws, and succession laws.

Many of the discriminatory provisions in the said areas of the law have fortunately been declared unconstitutional by the same court. They were glaringly in conflict with the Constitution which guarantees equality of spouses during marriage and at its dissolution, and outlaws discrimination on grounds of gender, among others.

They also conflicted with international conventions ratified by Uganda, like the Convention on the Elimination of All Forms of Discrimination Against Women.

Unfortunately, our patriarchal society, men and women alike, have been socialised into not questioning men's proprietory rights over women's bodies.

"Though the effect of the ruling was decriminalisation of adultery, it does not in the least legalise it."

That is why the average "Nakkus" will continue to publicly and proudly acknowledge being "wives" of monogamously-married men without considering the legal and criminal implications of their statements; or why the institution of polygamy will continue to be encouraged even by the very people who should shun it—the wives; or why some wives who are not beaten by their spouses will wonder whether they are loved; or why wives will ask their husbands "Wangula meka" (how much bride price did you pay for me) as an apparent challenge that they do not own them if they did not pay bride price to their parents; or why female genital mutilation continues to be endured by women; or why the enactment of the Domestic Relations Bill into law continues to be "a thorn in the flesh" for some sections of society including some legislators. The list is endless.

Removing Criminal Charges from Adultery Raises Questions

The second aspect of the ruling is the resultant creation of a lacuna (vacuum, gap) in as far as criminal adultery is concerned. Adultery ceased to be a crime when the ruling was made. While some sections of society have jubilated that they are now free to indulge in extramarital affairs, others are mourning that it is the end of morality, and the beginning of the law of the jungle on the issue. Both groups could have misinterpreted the position.

Though the effect of the ruling was decriminalisation of adultery, it does not in the least legalise it. Decriminalisation merely means that no one will be prosecuted in a criminal court and be punished on conviction. No law (or court decision for that matter) states that people must commit adultery, for that is what legalising adultery would mean.

Adultery still remains a matrimonial wrong that can be relied on as a ground for judicial separation or divorce, or even as a ground for claiming damages in civil courts if a party proves that he/she was injured by the adulterous conduct of a spouse. The definition of civil adultery is not discriminatory (gender neutral).

Recent court decisions have defined it to mean consensual sexual intercourse during subsistence of marriage between one spouse and a person of the opposite sex, not being a spouse. In simple language it means voluntary sexual intercourse between a married person and a person who is not a wife or husband of that married person.

Those who argue that adultery must remain criminal because it is immoral may need to know that not all immoral wrongs are criminal. The Ten Commandments are a good example.

A violation of some of them, like not going to church on the Sabbath Day/Sunday; not honouring your parents; adoring smaller gods other than the Almighty; coveting other people's property, etc, may be morally wrong but not necessarily criminal.

The bishop or pastor at you local church may declare you a sinner and probably condemn you to Hell for breaching the said commandments, or a practicing Catholic may confess them as sins before the priest, but no police officer will come knocking on your door for investigation and eventual prosecution.

Even some aspects of the Commandment—Thou shall not commit adultery—have not been criminalised in Uganda though they remain "sins" or moral wrongs. This is the aspect where two consenting adults, who are not married to anyone or to each other, indulge in voluntary sexual intercourse.

Such type of fornication remains a cardinal sin in the Bible but it is not a crime under our penal system. It only becomes a crime where one or both of the parties are not adults (defilement) or where the sexual union is forceful (rape) or is "unnatural" (bestiality, homosexuality) or, until the court ruling, where sexual rights of some third party have been violated (adultery).

The Pros and Cons of Criminalising Adultery

Various justifications have been advanced for criminalizing adultery.

These include the upholding of moral values, deterrence, punishment of offenders, and minimising the possibility of people taking the law in their own hands. All these are valid

Cheating Is Commonplace in Some Areas

While it's impossible to get an exact measure of infidelity, there are some clues about where the most cheating goes on. Beginning in the 1990s, researchers tracking the spread of HIV began extensively mapping sexual behavior in Sub-Saharan Africa. Their findings were astonishing: In the tiny West African nation of Togo, with a population of less than 6 million, 37 percent of married or cohabiting men said they've had more than one sex partner in the last year (the figure includes polygamists). Trailing just behind the Togolese were men in Cameroon, the Ivory Coast, Mozambique and Tanzania. In South Africa, even the AIDS educator at a Cape Town metal company told me that of course he had a girlfriend as well as a wife.

Pamela Druckerman, Lust in Translation: Which Country Has the Highest Rates of Infidelity? *New York: Penguin, 2007.*

religious and social justifications geared towards the protection of the sanctity of marriage as an age old institution. The paradox, however, is that the very same situation of criminalizing adultery could have the effect of destroying a marriage.

A spouse convicted of adultery at the instigation of his/her spouse (and for that matter, serving a jail sentence or paying compensation or a fine) may find it more difficult to reconcile than one who has merely been forgiven by the aggrieved spouse. A bruised ego is hard to nurse (especially the male ego?). In that light, decriminalising adultery and leaving spouses to mutually sort out their differences would be healthy for the sustenance of the marriage institution, which thrives on compromises, tolerance, and forgiveness.

Even the so called civil adultery need not be an automatic gateway to securing a divorce (ending a marriage) unless the marriage has reached a point of not being saved.

A common example is where the spouses have separated and each is cohabiting, and has children, with other parties. In some countries the principle is referred to as irretrievable breakdown of marriage and is a ground for divorce.

Periodical Bibliography

The following articles have been selected to supplement the diverse views presented in this chapter.

Zainah Anwar   "Stop the Moral Panic About Sex," *New Straits Times* (Malaysia), March 16, 2007.

Daniel J. DeNoon   "World Sex Survey Reveals Surprises," October 31, 2006. www.webmd.com.

Amrit Dhillon   "India's Antique Adultery Law Under Pressure to Change," *The Age* (Melbourne, Australia), April 14, 2007.

Durex   "Durex Global Sex Survey 2005," www.durex.com.

Justin McCurry   "International: No Sex, Thank You . . . We're Japanese," *The Observer* (England), March 30, 2008.

The Monitor (Kampala)   "Africa; 'Marriage Not a Barrier to Catching HIV/Aids,'" September 10, 2007.

The Monitor (Kampala)   "Uganda; 52 Per Cent of Kayunga Women Engage in Extra-Marital Sex," October 17, 2007.

The Nation   "Kenya; Court Ruling On Adultery Makes Two Wrongs Right," April 14, 2007.

New Vision   "Uganda; Will the New Adultery Law Be Fair to Both Men And Women?" April 15, 2007.

Pongphon Sarnsamak   "HIV Rate Rises in Married Couples," *The Nation* (Thailand), October 11, 2007.

Michael Sheridan   "Chaste China Dallies with a Sex Revolution," *The Sunday Times* (London), June 10, 2007.

The Statesman   (India), "Have We Come of Age?" November 1, 2006.

UN Integrated Regional Information Networks   "Africa; Sharing More than Just the Matrimonial Bed," June 20, 2007.

For Further Discussion

Chapter 1

The 1961 Dowry Prohibition Act aimed to put an end to the suffering of many Indian women whose husbands and in-laws demanded dowry. Unfortunately, the tradition of dowry, as well as the pressures and threats that are often attached to it, still exist. Some Indian men, however, claim that some women misuse the Act by falsely accusing their husbands and in-laws of demanding dowry. Using examples from Viewpoints 4 and 5, write a brief argument for or against the Dowry Act while keeping in mind the human rights of a husband and wife in marriage.

Chapter 2

Arranged marriage, child marriage, and polygamy are vastly different in concept and level of controversy, though all have stigmas attached that provoke some people to question the validity of the marriages. Using examples from the viewpoints, make an argument for or against the validity of one of the three types of marriage found in this chapter.

Chapter 3

Throughout the world, same-sex marriage is still a controversial subject. As more countries make the unity legal, however, it is gaining acceptance. Using information from the viewpoints, list three examples in favor of same-sex marriage and three examples against same-sex marriage. Be sure to include the country where the viewpoint originated.

Chapter 4

Chapter 4 recognizes the significance of money in marriage. The role of economics in a marriage can take on many forms. For example, as explained in Viewpoint 3, it can take on the role of a prenuptial agreement, allowing those who want to marry to protect their property in case of divorce. Or, as identified in Viewpoint 4, men in some areas of Pakistan buy brides from their families, thus putting a market value on women. Using examples from the viewpoints in this chapter, compare and contrast two roles of money in marriage while identifying the world location where such scenarios are common.

Chapter 5

The evolution of sex in terms of marriage is constantly changing through a loosening and tightening of morals and social revolutions. Using two examples from this chapter, write a brief description of how sex and marriage in the twenty-first century are progressively evolving and, in contrast, describe two examples of how sex and marriage today have not advanced or have regressed. While writing your arguments for and against this issue, recognize the global location of your examples.

Organizations to Contact

The editors have compiled the following list of organizations concerned with the issues debated in this book. The descriptions are derived from materials provided by the organizations. All have publications or information available for interested readers. The list was compiled on the date of publication of the present volume; the information provided here may change. Readers need to remember that many organizations take several weeks or longer to respond to inquiries.

Advocates for Youth
2000 M Street NW, Suite 750, Washington, DC   20036
(202) 419-3420 • fax: (202) 419-1448
e-mail: information@advocatesforyouth.org
Web Site: www.advocatesforyouth.org

Established in 1980, Advocates for Youth is an organization that works within the United States and developing countries with a mission to promote sexual and reproductive health education among adolescents. The organization promotes contraceptive use, the right for accurate sex education for adolescents, respect for young people's ability to make informed decisions about sex, and society's responsibility to inform its youth about sexual health and sexually transmitted diseases. The organization opposes abstinence-only-until-marriage programs as recognized in an article titled "Abstinence-Only-Until-Marriage Programs: Ineffective, Unethical, and Poor Public Health."

American Association for Marriage and Family Therapy (AAMFT)
112 South Alfred Street, Alexandria, VA   22314
(703) 838-9808 • fax: (703) 838-9805
Web site: www.aamft.org

Founded in 1942, the American Association for Marriage and Family Therapy (AAMFT) represents more than twenty-four thousand marriage and family therapists while promoting further research and education in this field of therapy. AAMFT sets guidelines and requirements for graduate education, training, ethics, and clinical work in the field of marriage and family therapy. Some of AAMFT's regular publications include the *Journal of Marital and Family Therapy* and *Family Therapy Magazine.*

Foundation for Women's Health, Research and Development (FORWARD)

Unit 4, 765–767 Harrow Road, London   NW10 5NY
   United Kingdom
44 02089604000 • fax: 44 02089604014
Web site: www.forwarduk.org

Established in 1983 in the United Kingdom, the Foundation for Women's Health, Research and Development (FORWARD) is an international nongovernmental organization that has the purpose to promote, protect, and improve the sexual health and human rights of African females throughout the world. FORWARD strongly opposes and works to eradicate such issues as child marriage, forced marriage, and female genital mutilation among African women. One specific interest of the organization is to prevent the condition of fistula, which is often a result of female genital mutilation and early pregnancy due to child marriage. FORWARD includes publications on their Web site and has organized an online "Forum on Marriage and the Rights of Women and Girls."

Soulforce Q

2000 Grand Avenue, Unit 2, Minneapolis, MN   55405
(469) 867-5725 • fax: (612) 236-4696
e-mail: Q@soulforce.org

Soulforce Q is the youth division of Soulforce, Inc., an organization that aims to protect and expand the rights of gay, lesbian, bisexual, and transgender/transsexual (GLBT) people through nonviolent resistance. Soulforce Q believes that religious and political oppression stunts the development of rights for GLBT Americans such as the freedom to marry anyone, regardless of gender. Soulforce Q publications include *Soulforce: A Brief History, 1999–2006* and an article found on their Web site titled "Right to Marry Campaign."

United Nations Children's Fund (UNICEF)
3 United Nations Plaza, New York, NY   10017
(212) 326-7000
Web site: www.unicef.org

The United Nations Children's Fund, or UNICEF, was created in 1946 to provide health care and food to needy children of the world, and emphasizes the importance of child development, education, gender equality, and the rights of children. UNICEF opposes and works to end such practices as child marriage, virginity testing, and female genital mutilation. One UNICEF sponsored project is the Kishori Abhijan project, which has a purpose to strengthen the education and self-esteem of teenagers, particularly girls, with the intention of promoting independent decision-making in the face of such issues as child marriage. Annually, UNICEF publishes "The State of the World's Children," which is a statistical report on children in 195 countries and territories.

United Nations Development Fund for Women (UNIFEM)
304 East Forty-Fifth Street, 15th Floor, New York, NY   10017
(212) 906-6400 • fax: (212) 906-6705
Web site: www.unifem.org

The United Nations Development Fund for Women (UNIFEM) supports programs that promote gender equality and female empowerment with a purpose to uphold and improve the human rights of women globally. UNIFEM aims to deplete poverty among females, eradicate violence against women, stop the expansion of AIDS among females, and to attain gender equality. UNIFEM publishes papers and pamphlets relating to women's human rights such as *Eliminating Female Genital Mutilation* and "Facts and Figures on Violence Against Women."

Women Living Under Muslim Laws (WLUML)

International Coordination Office, PO Box 28445
London   N19 5NZ
  United Kingdom
e-mail: wluml@wluml.org
Web site: www.wluml.org

Women Living Under Muslim Laws (WLUML) focuses on strengthening the human rights and equality of Muslim women. WLUML opposes the belief that there is one uniform Muslim world. Instead, WLUML believes that what are referred to as Muslim laws differ depending on such aspects as situation and location. Further, WLUML represents the opinion that Muslim laws were created through an array of perspectives, including religious, secular, and cultural. WLUML has published such articles as "South Africa: Divorcée Challenging Muslim Marriage" and "France: French Courts Annul Marriage Because Bride Was Not a Virgin."

World Health Organization (WHO)

Avenue Appia 20, Geneva 27   CH-1211
  Switzerland
41 227912111 • fax: 41 227913111
e-mail: info@who.int
Web site: www.who.int

Formed in 1948 through the United Nations, the World Health Organization (WHO) has the purpose of providing education and leadership on global public health issues with the mission for all people to possess the greatest level of health possible. WHO's agenda for improving public health includes such actions as promoting development and health security, reinforcing health systems, and utilizing research. WHO opposes child marriage while recognizing the health risks involved. Such risks are recognized in the WHO article "Early Marriage and Childbearing: Risks and Consequences."

Bibliography of Books

Flavia Agnes, Sudhir Chandra, and Monmayee Basu
Women and Law in India: An Omnibus Comprising Law and Gender Inequality, Enslaved Daughters, Hindu Women and Marriage Law. New York: Oxford University Press, 2004.

Prem Chowdhry
Contentious Marriages, Eloping Couples: Gender, Caste and Patriarchy in Northern India. New York: Oxford University Press, 2007.

Nicole Constable
Romance on a Global Stage: Pen Pals, Virtual Ethnography, and "Mail Order" Marriages. Berkeley, CA: University of California Press, 2003.

Stephanie Coontz
Marriage, a History: From Obedience to Intimacy, or How Love Conquered Marriage. New York: Viking Penguin, 2005.

Curzon
Sex & Marriage (The World of Sex: Perspectives on Japan and the West). London: RoutledgeCurzon Publishing, 2004.

Douglas Farrow and Daniel Cere
Divorcing Marriage: Unveiling the Dangers in Canada's New Social Experiment. Quebec: McGill-Queen's University Press, 2004.

Sara L. Friedman
Intimate Politics: Marriage, the Market, and State Power in Southeastern China. Cambridge, MA: Harvard University Asia Center, 2006.

Evan Gerstmann   *Same-Sex Marriage and the Constitution.* Cambridge, MA: Cambridge University Press, 2008.

Ladislav Holy   *Kinship, Honour, and Solidarity: Cousin Marriage in the Middle East.* Manchester, UK: Manchester University Press, 1989.

Jennifer Lee Huffman   *Money and Marriage: Choices, Rights and Responsibilities.* Petoskey, MI: Torch Lake Publishing, 1999.

Henry Neville Hutchinson   *Marriage Customs in Many Lands.* Whitefish, MT: Kessinger Publishing, 2005.

Kay S. Hymowitz   *Marriage and Caste in America: Separate and Unequal Families in a Post-Marital Age.* Chicago, IL: Ivan R. Dee, 2006.

Marion A. Kaplan   *Marriage Bargain: Women and Dowries in European History.* London: Routledge Mental Health, 1985.

Andrew Koppelman   *Same Sex, Different States: When Same-Sex Marriages Cross State Lines.* New Haven, CT: Yale University Press, 2006.

Herbert Mortimer Luckock   *The History of Marriage, Jewish and Christian in Relation to Divorce and Certain Forbidden Degrees.* Whitefish, MT: Kessinger Publishing, 2004.

Andrew R. Morrison and María Loreto Biehl — *Too Close to Home; Domestic Violence in Latin America.* Washington, DC: Inter-American Development Bank, 1999.

Veena Talwar Oldenburg — *Dowry Murder: The Imperial Origins of a Cultural Crime.* Oxford: Oxford University Press, 2002.

Daniel R. Pinello — *America's Struggle for Same-Sex Marriage.* New York: Cambridge University Press, 2006.

Mark Rebick — *The Changing Japanese Family.* London: Routledge, 2006.

Jaya Sagade — *Child Marriage in India: Socio-legal and Human Rights Dimensions.* Oxford: Oxford University Press, 2005.

Irene Spencer — *Shattered Dreams: My Life as a Polygamist's Wife.* Nashville, TN: Center Street, 2007.

Nancy Tapper — *Bartered Brides: Politics, Gender and Marriage in an Afghan Tribal Society.* Cambridge, MA: Cambridge University Press, 1991.

Arland Thornton, William G. Axinn, and Yu Xie — *Marriage and Cohabitation.* Chicago, IL: University of Chicago Press, 2007.

Noriko O. Tsuya and Larry L. Bumpass — *Marriage, Work, and Family Life in Comparative Perspective: Japan, South Korea, and the United States.* Honolulu, HI: University of Hawaii Press, 2004.

Ruth Vanita	*Love's Rite: Same-Sex Marriage in India and the West.* New York: Palgrave Macmillan, 2005.
Lynn Visson	*Wedded Strangers: The Challenges of Russian-American Marriages.* New York: Hippocrene Books, 2001.
Elissa Wall and Lisa Pulitzer	*Stolen Innocence: My Story of Growing Up in a Polygamous Sect, Becoming a Teenage Bride, and Breaking Free of Warren Jeffs.* New York: HarperCollins, 2008.
Robin West	*Marriage, Sexuality, and Gender.* Boulder, CO: Paradigm Publishers, 2007.
John Witte Jr.	*From Sacrament to Contract: Marriage, Religion, and Law in the Western Tradition.* Louisville, KY: Westminster John Knox Press, 1997.
K.P. Yadav	*Child Marriage in India.* New Delhi, India: Adhyayan Publishers & Distributors, 2006.
Sun-pong Yuen, Pui-Lam Law, Yuk-Ying Ho, and Fong-ying Yu	*Marriage, Gender, and Sex in a Contemporary Chinese Village.* Armonk, NY: M.E. Sharpe, 2004.

Index

Geographic headings and page numbers in **boldface** refer to viewpoints about that country or region.